How to Become a Successful
Actor
AND
Model

*To Ed,
Best wishes
Aaron*

Copyright © 2016 by Aaron Marcus
First published 2016 by the Marcus Institute
(410) 764-8270
All rights reserved. No part of this book may be reproduced, stored in a retrieval system, or transmitted, in any form or by any means—graphic, electronic, mechanical, photocopying, recording, or otherwise—without written permission of Aaron Marcus.
ISBN 978-0-9653585-3-8

Table of Contents

Introduction 1

1 What Is Commercial Modeling? 3
   What are commercial models used for? 3
   How much do commercial models earn? 3
   What does it take to make it as a commercial model? 4
   How do models get work? 4
   What are the advantages to working as a commercial model? 4
   What are the disadvantages? 4
   What does it take to get started? 5

2 Preparation for Commercial Modeling 7
   Acting lessons 7
   Looking comfortable in front of a still camera 15

3 Head Shots 17
   Tips for creating an eye-catching head shot 17

4 Resumes 19
   How to attach your resume to your head shot 21

5 Composite Sheets 23
   Putting together your composite sheet 25
   Studying successful models' composite sheets/photos 25
   Finding the right look for you 25
   Planning your shot 26
   Finding and hiring a photographer 27
   Things to consider when choosing a photographer 30
      What are the fees? 32
      Does the fee include a makeup artist, or does the model have to pay for one 32
      Can you meet with the photographer in person before the session? ..32
      Will you get black-and-white or color photos? 32
      How many photos will be taken? 32
      What will you receive after the shoot? 32
      Will the photographer select any photos? 33
      Who owns the rights to the photos? 33

      How long will it take to see your photos? 33
      Will a fee be charged if you are not happy with the photos and
      need to reshoot? 33
      How should you handle the photographers' fees? 33
      Are there additional photography services? 33
  Hiring a makeup artist 34
  Before the session 35
  After the session 35
  Designing and printing your composite sheet 37
  How many comps should you order? 38
  The ingredients of a professional composite sheet 39
  Composite sheets for children 40

6 Makeup **41**
  Basic List of Items You Need to Bring to a Set 42
  Additional items to bring to a shoot 43

7 Finding a Good Agent **45**
  Fees for agents 45
  Listings of agents 46
  Contacting agents 46
  Sample cover letter 47
  Make sure your materials are seen 48
  Make sure the agent is legitimate 49
  Signing with an agent 51
  Getting an agent's attention 52
  Managers and casting directors 52

8 How to Get Work **53**
  Agency websites 53
  Selling yourself 53
  Staying in touch with your agent 55
  Portfolios 55
  Working in other media 56
  Go-see 56
  Sample model form 57
  Layout 58
  How to take a better photo 61
  Conflicts 61
  Castings 62

Information you'll need after accepting a booking 62
Agent submittance 63
Agent's website 63
Direct bookings 63

9 How to Work as a Professional Model 65
What is expected of a professional model? 65
Be responsible 66
You were hired to model 67
Wardrobe 67
  How to get wardrobe you do not own 68
  Food and wardrobe do not mix 68
  Think before you speak 68
When to put on makeup 69
On the set 69
  Do not touch the props 69
  Getting information about the ad 69
  Getting conflicting information about the ad 70
Never discuss fees 70
Do not discuss upgrades while working 71
Let your agent renegotiate fees 71
The voucher 71
  Computing the time for the voucher. 73
The model release 74
Asking for a tear sheet 76
Information needed from every job 76
The work after the work 77
Keep all of your vouchers together 78
Turning down jobs 78
  Personal reasons 78
  Financial reasons 78
Two agents—two bookings—same day 80
When to call an agent 80
When you are unavailable for work 81
How to speak to an agent when work is slow 81
Additional modeling fees 82

10 Auditioning 83
Preparing for the audition 83
TV audition 83

Film audition 84
Radio and TV commercial audition 84
Physical auditioning techniques 85
   Where is your eye line? 85
Studying the sides 85
The Five W's 86
Memorizing scripts 86
Nervousness 87
   Mental exercise 87
   My three audition goals 88
   Physical exercises 88
Secrets to auditioning 88
   The casting office 89
   Questions for the casting director 89
   Slating 89
   Making mistakes 90
   Apologizing 90
   Nothing personal 90
On-camera home auditions 91
Equipment for home on-camera auditions 91
   Buying the equipment 93
   Programs for editing videos 93
   Voice-over software 93
   Microphones for audio recordings 93
How to position yourself during your audition 93
Don't over shoot 94
Uploading your audition 94
Better to audition with a casting director .95

11 The Realities of Being a Full-Time Actor and Model 97
Being self-employed 97
Is acting and commercial modeling for you? 97

12 Now What Do You Do? 101

13 Resources 103
Glossary of Terms 107
About the Author 117

Read This Before Beginning the Book

I would like to thank and congratulate you for purchasing this book. You have now taken the most important step in getting the needed information to become a successful actor and model.

As of this printing I have condensed 31 years of my experiences as a full-time working actor and commercial model into a practical, informative, enjoyable and valuable book that will greatly benefit you in your pursuit of acting and/or modeling as either a hobby or a full-time occupation.

While reading the book, please think of questions that you would like to have answered. They can be general questions about the industry or specific ones that pertain to improving your career. I will try to personally answer as many questions as possible.

You and I will greatly benefit from this individualized service. I am offering you a free, honest and straightforward response to your questions. In return, your questions will teach me what additional information is desired. This allows me to keep my in-person Book the Job seminars, online monthly workshops and the *Tear Sheet* newsletter up-to-date and informative.

If you would like more information about my in-person workshops, online webinars or on-line mentoring programs or the *Tear Sheet* newsletter, simply visit my website at www.howtoactandmodel.org. You can also reach me at (410) 764-8270.

To get your list of agents throughout the United States, just e-mail me (aaron@howtoactandmodel.com) the date, location and state of your book purchase, and I will e-mail you the link for the listing. You will also be added to my special mailing list and receive free acting and modeling information.

Thanks again for your purchase, and I hope you enjoy this book.

Sincerely,

Aaron Marcus

Aaron Marcus

For Nancy

Acknowledgments

Cover Photo: David Blecman—www.posneg.com

Models: Molly Horton and Jeff Moore

Makeup Artist: Sana Cordeaux

Jeremy & Jennifer,
thank you for being the most wonderful children any dad could ask for.

A special thank you to Laurie Mazur. I can't thank you enough for
all of your help and support.

Introduction

When most people think of modeling, they only think of *fashion* models—those tall, thin, glamorous men and women who appear in ads for designer clothes. But you don't need to look like Tyra Banks, Gisele Bündchen, Cindy Crawford or Edward Wilding to succeed as a model. *Commercial* models, who appear in ads for everything from toothpaste to insurance, come in all shapes, sizes and ages. Some are gorgeous and handsome; however, many successful commercial models look just like everyday people. The individual who has the greatest chance of being chosen to appear in an ad is the one who can believably look like a mom, doctor, businessperson, plumber, student, grandparent, teacher, dad, etc. Although there are many beautiful and handsome commercial models, it is not necessary to have that "perfect" look in order to be successful. This book will explain the best ways to:

- Get started—by teaching you specific techniques to help you practice looking comfortable and believable in front of the camera
- Make contacts—by showing you how to find literally thousands of agents, photographers, websites and art/creative directors
- Grab the attention of agents—by helping you discover what agents want to see in head shots and commercial photos
- Learn techniques—to help you get cast in acting and modeling projects
- Market yourself—and work on your own
- Accurately manage the business side—and understand how the industry works
- Learn the tricks to auditioning—and how to shoot auditions at home
- Understand industry terminology—with a handy glossary at the back of the book

As in any business, there are no guarantees in the acting and modeling industry. However, being prepared and extremely knowledgeable gives you the greatest chance for success.

ONE
What Is Commercial Modeling?

What Are Commercial Models Used For?
Every day you see commercial models in many different types of ads. They appear in newspapers, catalogs, magazines, editorials (photos shown in conjunction with an article in a magazine), brochures and on posters, billboards, sides of buses, packages of food items, household products, websites, etc.

The commercial model is the silent salesperson promoting a product or company. He or she has to act without words.

To even be considered as a *fashion* model, you must meet very specific physical requirements. Normally female fashion models are between 5'9" and 6'0" tall have a 34-inch bust, 24-inch waist and 34-inch hip. Some markets outside of the United States will allow the models to be a little shorter. Male fashion models are normally 6'0" to 6'2" tall, wear a size 40 regular or long jacket and have a 30–32 size waist.

Commercial models, on the other hand, need only to have the ability to look like a real person. In commercial modeling people of all heights, weights, sizes, ages, and races are hired. Fashion models normally promote high-end designer clothes; commercial models advertise everything else. There are some agencies that will only work with women who are a minimum of 5'6" or 5'7" or taller, but many do not have any restrictions.

The commercial model connects the client, the product and the consumer. A client is the person whose product needs to be advertised. Usually, the client hires an ad agency to produce an ad, the ad agency hires the photographer, and either the art/creative director from the ad agency or photographer hires the commercial model through the model's agent.

How Much Do Commercial Models Earn?
The fees are different from city to city and job to job. Adult commercial models can expect to make anywhere from $50 to $250 an hour depending on the market. Children are paid less than adults but can earn up to $75 an hour. There is no way of knowing how much one can earn. I know a commercial

model who earned $50,000 from one job, and I know people who have made $2,000 for an entire year.

Most people do not realize that commercial modeling is like any other kind of business. Before entering this or any industry, you must do your homework. You must learn about the types of photos that will get you the most work. You must understand what agents do and must know how to make sure you are working with a reputable and honest agent. You must know what is expected of you as a professional model and learn how to practice before entering the business. Certainly, the people who have done their research and have gotten the needed information will have the greatest chance for success.

What Does It Take to Make It as a Commercial Model?
The best way to get work as a commercial model is to learn some basic acting skills, be self-motivated, and have the time to accept work.

How Do Models Get Work?
Although this process is explained in greater detail later in the book, the short answer is that agents can e-mail JPEGs of your photos directly to a photographer or art/creative director, and they decide which model to hire for the job. Or, the agents can have people visit their websites to see your images. Sometimes models audition for the job by attending a go-see. This is when models go to a photographer's studio or casting office and audition in person.

What Are the Advantages to Working as a Commercial Model?
As I mentioned earlier, there are no physical limitations to being a commercial model. Most people do commercial modeling on a part-time basis. Not only is it so much fun to be shot by a professional photographer, but it is also thrilling to see yourself or your child in a magazine, newspaper, website, billboard or poster. The hours are extremely flexible, and the fees paid to commercial models are incredible.

What Are the Disadvantages?
There is no guarantee that there will be steady work. That is why most people work part-time. There are no health benefits, and no money is withheld from your checks for tax purposes. You are responsible for paying taxes on all income.

What Does It Take to Get Started?
A person can get started by simply having a head shot taken. Later in the book I explain how to get photos taken free as well as how to find professional photographers to shoot your head shots. Depending on the area, one can have a head shot taken and begin trying to get work for an average cost of $250–$500. Finding agents to submit your head shot for jobs would be the best next step. It is important to get experience working in front of a camera before trying to work in a major market.

TWO
Preparation for Commercial Modeling

Acting Lessons
A commercial model must be able to act without words. Acting lessons can give you the tools. Acting lessons can teach you how to reexperience emotions, to re-create events and situations from your past, and to bring them to the present. You must be able to feel emotions in front of a camera and quickly switch them.

I am going to discuss some acting tips later in this book, but I would like to share one technique that helps me get into character while working with a photographer. The technique involves saying a word or short phrase (that helps you grab the needed emotion) to yourself or the other model while shooting.

Talk about the product. Bring the words and message of the ad alive with your actions. For example, you are doing an ad for insulation. The ad is trying to convey that when you use insulation in your home, you feel warmer in the winter and cooler in the summer and your utility bills will be lower. You are holding a package of insulation in your hands, and you might say one of these short phrases: "This stuff is great. My house stays so warm. My heating bill is lower. It's incredible." The way to make yourself believe what you are saying, which will make everyone looking at the ad believe you, is to connect the words with something real in your life. Even if insulation does not matter to you, there is something that you own or would like to own that will make you more comfortable. Think of that object during the shoot.

If talking is not appropriate, then think the words to yourself. Imagine you are working on an ad where a bank wants to show how pleasant, friendly and helpful its employees are. Your character is the customer at the other bank in town. You can't get your questions answered. It takes a long time before someone even tries to help you. Try to remember a real experience where you were not treated well. If you are asked to show a certain emotion about something you have never experienced, then you should remember an experience that will give you the same emotion, even though it might not connect to the product.

One of the exciting things about commercial modeling is being able to play different characters. One day you can be a nerd, and the next day, the president of a corporation.

Commercial models must be able to understand the concept of an ad, take direction from an art/creative director or photographer and produce the look on the spot. I had to show a variety of emotions during the shoot in the next two ads you see.

A nationally known science museum was promoting a film called *Antarctica*. In the ad you see a man (me) dressed for summer. I am wearing a Hawaiian shirt and watching the *Antarctica* film. The film is so realistic that you feel like you are there.

Because it is so cold in Antarctica, I have a windburned face, ice forming on my mustache, and snow on my feet. Penguins are standing next to me.

Here is the tricky part. If I look like I am freezing, the shot doesn't work. The museum doesn't want people to think that they will feel uncomfortable if they attend the film. The photographer wanted me to look cold, but in a pleasant way.

How did I do that? I brought back memories of wonderful times I had in very cold environments: skiing, sledding, playing with my family in the snow. The next page shows the final ad.

Preparation for Commrcial Modeling • 9

Photo by Steve Pollock - Franklin Institute

Here's another example of the need to show different emotions. This was an editorial photo for *Maxim* magazine. Yes, I know people don't normally think of someone looking like me being in that type of magazine. But, the article was about how long men live. It listed predictors of a man's life span depending on his eating, sleeping and exercise habits. To make the article more enjoyable to read, they hired me to be the funeral home director. Depending on your lifestyle habits, I would "size you up" to determine how long you would live. They wanted a scary almost ghoulish type of look. I tapped into events from my past where I felt those angry, scary, evil emotions.

The next following pages show samples from different jobs where many types of emotions were needed.

Photo by John Devine—As it originally appeared in *Maxim* magazine

If you are ever working with an animal, always ask if it is a professionally trained animal. If it is not, you run a much higher risk of an accident taking place on the set. The capuchin monkey in this photo bit the assistant photographer. As it turned out, the monkey was just a pet and not properly trained.

Photo by Tony Sylvestro

Sometimes models are asked to show a caricature or highly exaggerated look instead of a real expression. That means making the character look almost cartoonish. Emotions must be blown up to such a level that the anger, frustration or happiness looks humorous or silly.

Here is a photo for an ad using a caricature format.

To do a caricature, you must be able to reproduce the basic feeling, then completely let go and make the shot look cartoonish. The photographer or art/creative director will let you know if you are heading in the right direction.

The following two pages show examples of different types of emotions used for jobs.

Photo by Clark Vandergrift - Air Products

TRG Reality, Cleveland Ohio

Preparation for Commercial Modeling • 13

Photo by David Blecman

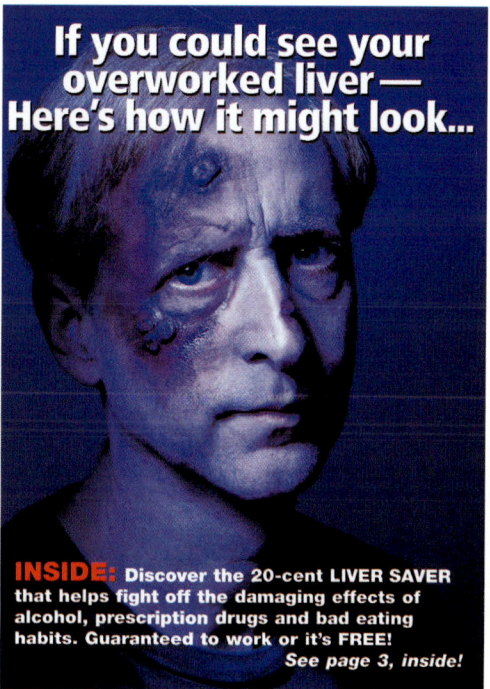

Photo by Larry Ruggeri

Photo by Bob Vergara

14 • *How to Become a Successful Actor and Model*

Photo by Scot Gordon

Godfrey Advertising

Photo by Len Rizzi

Photo By Clark Vandergrift

Having the ability to show a variety of expressions and emotions will give you many more opportunities to get cast in various projects.

Looking Comfortable in Front of a Still Camera

To help yourself practice looking comfortable and believable in front of the camera, make a list of different expressions and emotions. The most commonly used expressions in advertising are happiness, anger, frustration, love, feeling sick, confusion, and caring. Then, think of situations that will help you feel them. For example, if I wanted to practice looking happy, I would need to ask myself what kind of happiness I am feeling. Am I happy because I won the $20 million lottery, or because I got an A on my exam, or because I just got engaged? Next, I would think of an experience from my past that would allow me to feel the emotion needed for the proper look. If I needed to feel the excitement of winning a race, I could think about the time I hit a grand slam in a Little League all-star game. If you do not have any appropriate experiences, use your imagination.

Now that you have a list of emotions and have figured out ways of retrieving them, the next step is to have a friend or relative take pictures of you. You can use any kind of camera; anything from a digital camera to a cell phone will do for this exercise. Just make sure that the photos are clear and your body and face can be easily seen. Have the list of emotions nearby, and work on one at a time. Try to remember the situation that will put you in touch with that feeling. Study the photos and see where you were successful and where more work is needed.

Here are some other helpful techniques to use while practicing. It is best to look away from the camera while you are preparing yourself. That way there is less chance of the photographer accidentally taking your photo before you are ready, and it is easier to concentrate. Look at the ground or at a wall away from the camera. When you are ready, look straight into the lens of the camera. When you are on a professional modeling job, there will be times when the photographer asks you not to look directly into the lens, but most of the time models are asked to look straight into the camera. If you are planning to look away from the camera, make sure you find a spot to use as a landmark, so you can get your head in precisely the same position after each photo is taken. If you want to look just to the left of the camera, then find a place on the wall, or the edge of the camera, to use as your mark. Whenever you look away from the lens, it is very difficult to consistently place your head in the same spot without a focus point.

Take acting classes and perform in local theater. This will help you learn techniques that allow you to grab hold of different feelings. Mastering these skills will give you many different looks. Having access to a wide variety of expressions will make work enjoyable and challenging. Being able to take direction and translate thoughts and feelings into facial and body expressions will make you a more versatile and marketable model.

THREE
Head Shots

The next step in becoming a commercial model is to have a head shot taken. Head shots are generally close-up photos of your face from your chest to the top of your head. Some people get commercial modeling jobs with only a head shot. In fact, that is how I got started.

Composite sheets, the model's business card, which are discussed later, will generally have one head shot photo. Also, many commercial models work as actors, and head shots are an essential tool of their trade.

It is important to understand what is needed to produce a great commercial head shot. People want to see warm, inviting and approachable looks. Your head shot should capture your personality or the look of how others can see you being cast. If you also have a strong quirky type look, perhaps you could create two separate head shots showing off both looks. A commercial head shot should not be too dramatic.

Tips for Creating an Eye-Catching Head Shot
1. Figure out your type. How are you realistically going to be cast. It is good to be typecast.
2. Have a plain background. You don't want anything distracting people from looking at you.
3. Look directly into the lens of the camera. Looking even slightly away makes you look hidden and less approachable.
4. Have one shoulder slightly closer to the camera. It will give you a stronger presence.
5. Avoid jewelry and clothes that are distracting. Large stripes and patterns are distracting.
6. Your wardrobe should match and accentuate the look you need to achieve.
7. Do not have any logos or brand names on your clothing. It could keep you from working for the competitors of these companies.
8. Avoid showing too much skin on your arms and chest area. The viewers' eyes will focus on those areas.

9. Practice creating the emotions you need to show during the head shot session. This will help bring life into your eyes.
10. Pick out the right wardrobe and show it to the photographer, either in person or electronically.

In Chapter 5, I discuss how to find a photographer and the questions you need to ask prior to your session. But I will mention two things here.

Styles change, but today everyone, with a few exceptions, is using color head shots. 8 x 10 is the standard size.

Since most actors have their head shots uploaded to websites, it is crucial that your face jumps out on a monitor. That is why it is so important to always have a close-up shot and not a half or three-quarter body shot. Otherwise your face can hardly be seen very clearly.

Since many of the roles I am cast in are for the doctor, lawyer, teacher, therapist, someone you trust, like, will share personal information with, I made sure that I was thinking of people in my life who I truly care about during the photo session. That helps provide the warmth and openness you see in my eyes. You will also notice that the wardrobe fits these types of roles, and nothing is distracting or taking people away from looking at me.

Photo by Joe Henson

FOUR

Resumes

If you are interested in acting, you will need a one-page resume attached to the back of your 8 x 10 head shot.

Here is an example of what a resume should look like.

YOUR NAME
Union Affiliation (for example, SAG-AFTRA)
Your Phone Number (or agent's)
(optional) Google Voice Number
e-mail address
website address
www.imdb link (if you have an Internet Movie Data Base page)

Eyes: Blue
Hair: Blonde
Height: 6'0"
Weight: 158 lbs.

THEATER:

Name of Play	Character	Company/Theater or Director
Hamlet	Hamlet	Arena Stage

FEATURE/INDEPENDENT FILMS:

Name of Film	Character (type of role)	Studio or Director
Project Almanac	History Teacher – Supporting	Paramount Pictures

TELEVISION:

Name of Show	Character (type of role)	Network or Director
House of Cards	Michael (Butler) Co-Star	Netflix

COMMERCIALS—RADIO/TELEVISION:
List of Credits Available Upon Request

SPECIAL SKILLS:

Examples:
Martial Artist	Athlete (list sports)	Scuba Diver
Musician (list instruments)	Dancer (list styles)	Ride Motorcycle

TRAINING AND EDUCATION:

Examples:
B.S. (Theater)		University of Such and Such
Stanislavski Techniques:		Harry Stanis
Improv:		The Academy of Improv, NY
Acting for the Camera:		Jane Song

Size of the resume—Your resume has to be cut to 8 x 10 so that it cleanly fits on your head shot.

Head shot on your resume—Having a head shot (either the same one as on the other side or a different head shot) in the upper right-hand corner of your resume allows people to continue to see you as they read your resume.

Phone number—You can create a free business-related phone number by registering at www.google.com/voice. You can have calls forwarded to your cell phone and not give out your personal number.

Character type—You want to list the importance of the role you had in a project next to the character name. When you book the job, you can ask if you are a lead, co-star, guest starring, etc.

Extra work—I would not recommend placing extra work on your resume. It does not necessarily show any acting skills. If extra work is all you have done, then list it, but put the word "extra" beside the character description so no one thinks you are trying to fool them into thinking it was a principal role.

Listing of commercials—Typically, you don't want to list any TV or radio commercials on your resume. This is to avoid the appearance of "product conflicts"—where a person appears in ads for competing products. If you were in a commercial for Nike 10 years ago but had it listed on your resume, you might not be considered for a Reebok commercial, because of a perceived conflict. The casting director might think the spot is still airing. However, if nothing is listed and you are asked if you have any TV commercials currently running that would be considered a conflict to Reebok, you can honestly say no.

Special skills—Listing strong special skills can be invaluable to a casting director who is trying to find people with certain abilities. This is especially true for those with few credits on their resumes. Make the skills specific—don't just say horseback riding; list if you ride Western or English, etc. This lets the casting director know exactly what you can do, and it gives you more credibility.

Education—Make your listings as specific as possible. Don't just say Intro to Acting. That does not tell people what you studied. You can say Script Analysis, Commercial Acting, etc.

If you studied at a school that people will know, then list the school. If your teacher is known, then list the teacher's name. This will also be helpful if you have few credits. People will see that you are just getting started but have studied at good schools or with well-respected teachers.

How to attach your resume to your head shot
There are many ways you can attach your resume to your head shot. There is no one right way. I will share with you the pros and cons, and then you can decide which way is best for you:

1. Print it onto the back. If you are doing a small run for an event, then as long as the lettering does not bleed through the photo, this can work. The only problem is if you need to add more credits to your resume, you will have to throw the head shots away.
2. Glue your resume. This is messy, it is hard to get the paper lined up, and the resume can separate easily.
3. Use sticky paper that has glue on one side. This is expensive and also hard to line up properly.
4. Staple one or two corners. This allows people to take notes during an audition. The resume can easily separate from your head shot.
5. Staple all four corners to your head shot. This is what I do. It will not separate, and I can easily remove the staples and replace it with an updated resume. This allows me to keep the head shot.

As shown in the example, your resume should include your:
- Name (and possibly your agent's name)
- Union affiliation—The two most well-known unions for actors in the United States are SAG-AFTRA, www.sagaftra.org, and AEA Actors' Equity Association (theater), www.actorsequity.org. In Canada, the union is ACTRA Alliance of Canadian Cinema, Television and Radio Artists, www.actra.ca/main. For more information about unions, see Chapter 13: Resources. You can learn about additional unions by visiting my websie at www.howtoactandmodel.org and clicking on the resource tab.
- Height
- Weight
- Hair color
- Eye color
- Experience:

- Plays you have been in
- Corporate/educational, feature or independent films
- TV shows
- Training (where you have studied)
- Special skills (foreign languages, gymnastics, juggling, firearms, etc.)

When you are listing your special skills, you should include things other than acting experience. If you are a teacher, lawyer, veteran, doctor, police officer, mechanic, etc., make sure you put this information on your resume. If a film is being cast and police officers are needed, and your resume shows that you are a police officer, you may have a greater chance of being brought in to audition. When you are first beginning, you might not have much information to put on your resume. List anything: high school plays, community or college theater, or any relevant acting experience. If you worked on a play in an acting class, list it as a scene study. List all of your training. Showing your training credits (classes or seminars) can improve your chances of getting an audition even with little acting experience.

The only guideline is that you must be honest. Do not lie on your resume. A casting director once told me about an actor who came in to read for a part. She looked at his resume and noticed he had a certain play listed on his resume. It just so happened the casting director's husband had directed that play. She knew everyone in the cast and knew that he had not been in the play. She told him to leave her office and that he would never be allowed to audition for anything she was casting. So, don't fib about your experiences.

Similarly, only list special skills that you are proficient in. An agent once told me about a person who was cast for a job partly because she had listed riding horses as a special skill. While shooting the commercial, the director learned that the actor not only could not ride horses, but was scared to death of them. She was fired on the spot and immediately replaced.

Modeling jobs should not be listed on your acting resume. Your resume is a continuous work in progress. As you get more impressive jobs, or perhaps study with some well-known teachers, you will want to replace the old listings with the updated information.

Remember, resumes are used exclusively by actors trying to get acting jobs. Models do not use resumes. The head shot and resume are your most basic work tools. Next you will need a composite sheet.

FIVE
Composite Sheets

A composite sheet is a collection of photographs that shows the variety of ways you can look. The composite sheet, also known as the "comp" or "zed card," is one of the keys that unlocks the door to getting work. Since so much of our work is done electronically, some people don't feel the need to create a composite sheet. I think it is still essential that all commercial models have a card. You always want to bring a few cards with you when attending a go-see, in case the photographer is accepting them. And, you will use a comp card when marketing yourself to agents, photographers and art/creative directors at advertising agencies.

The most basic composite sheet will have a head shot on one side and two to four different photos on the back. I have also seen one-sided comp cards that have three to four photos only on the front with nothing on the back, and four-sided comp cards showing many photos. The most common size is 5 x 7. There are more samples on the next page.

2-sided Comp Card

24 • *How to Become a Successful Actor and Model*

Pages 1 and 4 of a 4-sided Comp Card

Pages 2 and 3 of a 4-sided Comp Card

There is no set rule on how a comp must look. The size, shape and appearance of a card is limited only by the model's imagination. However, you should ask what size card your agent prefers. A few agencies still keep comps in plastic bins attached to a wall. This makes it easy for them to see who should be submitted for jobs. If they have your comp card on their wall, you want to make sure that your card fits in the bin. If you are going to market yourself, then make sure you create a card that can easily fit into a mailing envelope.

Putting Together Your Composite Sheet
If you are just beginning in commercial modeling and do not have any photos for a composite sheet, or you have done some ads but aren't crazy about the shots, or you like the photos you have done but feel they are not selling you well, then you can create your own "ad" photos. Here's how.

Studying Successful Models' Composite Sheets/Photos
Ask agents and commercial photographers if they have any composite sheets in their files or commercial photos on their websites that they consider special.

Ask to see the photos of successful models. Get input from everyone, but remember, you are the one who should make the final decision. There are many printing companies that specialize in turning your commercial shots into comp cards. You can view the numerous styles and formats these printers offer. (In my *Industry Information Directory*, I list 17 printers. You can e-mail me to order the directory.)

Finding the Right Look for You
Deciding on the image or images that fit you best might be the hardest part of the whole process of putting together a composite sheet and commercial photos that market you well. Ask agents, casting directors, photographers, art/creative directors and friends how they see you being cast. Consider their input, but you need to make the final decision. You must figure out how you want to present yourself to the world. Are you a grandparent type? An athlete? Are you the student who is having problems studying for the SAT exam? Do you look right drinking beer around a campfire, or sitting behind an office desk—or both?

If appropriate for you, consider using some of the following "looks" on your card. These "types" are a few of the many character types you will see in commercial modeling ads:

Think about the types of photos that would best display those images. To help with ideas, look through:

- Banker
- Blue collar
- Body shots—if appropriate show hands, feet, legs, etc. (Some ads only show parts of the model's body.)
- Business (non-executive-manager type)
- Customer
- Dad, mom, grandparent
- Executive
- Exercise
- Family
- Housewife
- Nurse or doctor
- Outdoors
- Pharmaceutical (cold, cough, flu, etc.)
- Real estate agent
- Relationship (husband-wife, boyfriend-girlfriend, etc.)
- Salesperson
- Sports activity
- Student or teacher

- Magazine ads
- Newspaper ads
- Junk mail
- Agents' websites
- Stock photography websites (discussed later in this chapter)
- Photographers' showcase books/websites (photographers pay to have their work shown in books and on websites to generate business for themselves). One publication is called Workbook (www.workbook.com). You can see some beautiful photographs and perhaps get some ideas for shots that you can do.

Planning Your Shot

You want each shot to look like an ad for a specific company or product. Never use a logo or a brand name, for example, Nike or McDonald's, in your shot. It could prevent you from getting other jobs with a competitor. You don't want to have the same look in all of your photos. Let industry professionals see that you have the ability to show a wide variety of expressions by having a different emotion or look for each photo. Showing a wide range of expressions in various photos will allow you to be considered for more jobs than if you just had one specific look in every shot.

Since the shots for your composite sheet don't have words, make sure each photograph itself tells the story. Even better, create a photo that shows more than one story. If you want to present yourself as a mom and a businesswoman, the photo might show you walking up the steps to your house wearing a business suit, carrying a laptop bag, while your child runs to meet you. Take your time and be creative in thinking of different scenarios for your shots. When people can see you in a shot as a mom, then they are more open to casting you as a mom for an ad.

Magazines are a great source of ideas. Find the magazine that will feature the look you want. For example, *Parents* magazine is great for shots of parents and kids.

For business images, look through investment magazines. You can also visit stock photography websites for ideas. You can type in key words and search for stock shots showing photos for teacher, athlete, mom, real estate agent, etc. The key thing to remember is that many stock shots only look like ads when the copy (words), headline or product is added to the image. You need to find a shot that looks like an ad with no copy. Here are some well-known stock photography companies: https://us.fotolia.com, www.gettyimages.com, www.istockphoto.com. You can easily find others by doing a Google search for stock photography websites.

The magazine ads and stock shots can give you information on how to style the shot and what props are needed. Props are items placed on the set to make the ad look real. For example, if the ad is supposed to take place in an auto garage, then tools, oil cans, towels, grease guns, and auto parts would be appropriate props.

After selecting the types of shots you want, show the samples to anyone connected to the modeling, acting or advertising industry for feedback. If you have not contacted an agent, show your ideas to art directors at advertising agencies, or photographers. If you are trying to borrow ideas from an existing ad, do not expect to be able to make an exact duplicate. You probably will not have the money or experience. Do the best you can at making the shot look like a *real ad*.

Finding and Hiring a Photographer

Get the names of photographers working in your area. Ask agents, art/creative directors or other models and actors for the names of their favorite photographers. If you do not have any contacts, visit the American Society of Media Photographers website (http://asmp.org). Some ASMP members only photograph landscapes, wildlife or portraits, but many shoot ads with models. You can also search for assistant photographers. They might be looking for models to shoot in order to build up their portfolios. Here is another group you can look into: American Photographic Artists, http://apanational.org. I also suggest you look into finding photographers through Meetup, www.meetup.com. Search for photography Meetup groups in your area.

You might be able to get your photos free or at a reduced cost if the photographer is willing to do the shoot as a TFP (trade for print). No money is exchanged between the photographer and model for this arrangement. Some photographers like to do "test shots." Test shots are not ads, but they are used by the photographer and model for promotional purposes. Test shots can be free, but sometimes the photographer will charge the model a greatly reduced session fee.

Here is an example of a test shot. Although this photo was shot as a test, an art director saw it on my composite sheet, and he paid a fee so he could use it as an ad. Whether you hire a photographer for a photo session or do test shots, try to make the final product look like an ad.

Photo by Bill Schilling—Jeremy Marcus

Another way to get photos for your comp (and actually get paid) is to find a photographer who shoots stock photos. These are generic photographs that can be used for many purposes. Typical stock photos include images of a happy husband and wife looking at their newborn baby, or of a businessperson sitting at a desk. Companies use stock photography because it is less expensive to purchase (actually rent) a ready-made stock photo than to produce an original photograph.

WARNING! There are, however, a few things to keep in mind before appearing in a stock shot. When a model is hired for a regular ad, there are specific agreements on the amount of time the ad can run and where it will be used. The model is paid a specific amount of money based on that information. When a model is hired for a stock shot, he or she must sign a document allowing the photographer or stock company to run the photo anywhere and forever without the model receiving any additional fees. Your image could be used on billboards, posters or products. If you become closely identified with a certain product because of the ad in which a stock photo appears, you could lose out on other jobs for competing products. You can make money and get great tear sheets when doing stock shots, but you are taking the risk of possibly losing money in the future.

Another thing to consider before doing a stock shot is that you never know what type of ad your image may appear in. You could be portrayed as a drug addict, alcoholic, pregnant teenager, child abuser or some other character you might not want to be associated with. I was told about a model whose stock photo was used in a newspaper ad that showed her as one of the employees for a phone sex company.

When attending a go-see, sometimes you will be asked if you have done any ads for, let's say, insurance companies or pharmaceutical ads. With stock photography, you have no idea where your ad has run. This could create serious issues if you say you have not done any of these types of ads, you book a pharmaceutical job, and then the company sees your image in a stock shot for a competing product.

Many agents discourage models from doing stock photography. Some stock companies will hire models directly, so the agents lose out on their commissions. If the model becomes associated with a certain product, the agent could lose commissions on future bookings. If the model becomes closely associated with a sleazy or controversial ad, it might be very difficult for the agent to find photographers or art directors interested in hiring the model for future jobs. That will also mean less income for the agent.

I decided to do this stock shot because I knew that the photo would be so memorable that I would actually get more work from it. However, I have not done any since then, nor would I do any stock shots in the future.

If hiring a professional photographer is not in your budget at this time, use your creativity. I have known models who found college students taking photography classes to shoot the photos for their comps. The stu-

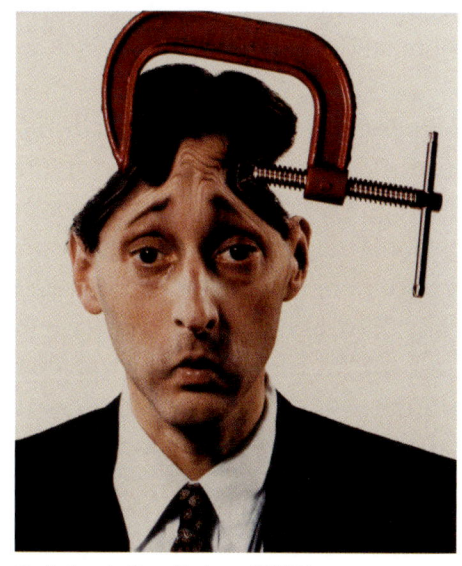

Stock photo by Barry Blackman, NY, NY

dents loved having access to models to work with, and the models got very nice photos at little or no cost. One student actually used the photos for a class project. There are no guarantees that the photos will be usable for your comp. However, you could spend $500 for a professional photo session and still not get exactly what you need. Even if the photos don't work, the session will build your experience. Another advantage of going this route is that you never know where the photographer might end up in the industry. The photographer might become very successful and want to hire you again. Just be careful. If you are shooting with a photographer who you found on your own, I believe it is important to bring someone with you to make sure the photographer is legit.

Another inexpensive way of getting shots taken is by calling a number of local photographers and asking if they can recommend any assistant photographers. Assistant photographers are people who work as apprentices to more established photographers. They help the photographer with adjusting lights, moving sets or anything needed during the shoot. Many are trying to build their portfolios in order to get their own bookings. They may be in great need of models to work with.

Set up appointments and interview a few photographers. Show the photographer ads that interest you. Clearly explain the look and concept of the shots you want. A photographer told me about a singer who was doing a shot for her album cover. The singer wanted a tough sexy look but did not make that clear to the photographer. Although the photographer made her look beautiful, the singer was unhappy with the photographs. Make sure the photographer really understands what you need.

Things to Consider When Choosing a Photographer

Notice how the photographer responds to your photo selections. Does the photographer have suggestions for how he or she sees you being cast?

Will the photographer shoot on location? "On location" means shooting your photos outside the photographer's studio—for instance, at a gym or bank, in your home or at the ocean or a ski resort. Try to shoot a few of your "test ads" in a few locations to help make the photos look like real ads. Ask around and see if you have access to a doctor's office, ball field, hospital, store, garage, library, school or restaurant. You might be surprised how helpful people can be when you approach them nicely and clearly explain to them that you are trying to put together shots for your composite sheet or portfolio. Make sure they understand that you are not producing an ad.

Normally, people are paid to have their facilities used for ads, or at least they get name credits in the ads. When shooting on location, make sure the person who is giving you permission to shoot knows exactly what the shot will look like. You do not want to run into a situation where the owner of a store doesn't feel comfortable with the type of shot you are doing and asks you to leave in the middle of the session. Clearly explain the type of shot, the approximate length of the session, and how many people will be involved. Ask when it would be most convenient for them. Don't disrupt any business that might be going on while you are shooting.

Leave the place looking even better than before you got there. Don't burn any bridges; you might want to go back there again at some point. Send a thank you note, and definitely send a copy of the shot and/or your composite sheet with the photo on it as a way of saying thanks.

With the photographer's permission, you can offer to let the establishment use your photo in an ad at no charge. If your shot won't work as an ad for the establishment, perhaps the photographer would agree to do one free publicity photo for the business. If the photographer is just getting started, doing a free photo could be a good way to make a contact and add to his or her portfolio. Make sure the shots can be done, both technically and within your budget.

Do you feel comfortable with the photographer? This is just as important as the quality of the photographer's work. You must be able to relax and try out ideas during a shoot, otherwise the camera will capture your anxiety, and your photos will show you looking uncomfortable. View the photographer's portfolio. See if he or she has taken any photos in the same style you desire. If not, you should not necessarily dismiss the photographer. Perhaps the photographer can do a wonderful job but has not had the opportunity to shoot in that particular style. The main thing to look for is the clarity and "life" in the shots. Are they in focus? Do the models look sharp and show personality? A sign of a good photo is that when you initially look at the picture, you immediately are attracted to the model's eyes. If the photos look clear but are not especially creative, don't worry. Remember, you are the one who will be bringing many ideas to the shot.

Before hiring a photographer to shoot your photos, make sure you get the following information:

What are the fees?
You can expect to pay anywhere from $150 to $800 for the session. Fees vary

depending on the package offered, types of shots, how many different looks will be shot and the location of the studio.

Does the fee include a makeup artist, or does the model have to pay for one?
The cost for a professional makeup artist can range from $50 to $200. The average fee in large markets is $150. For a discussion on whether you'll need a makeup artist, see the section Hiring a Makeup Artist later in this chapter.

Can you meet with the photographer in person before the session?
It is always best to meet with the photographer prior to the session. You will get a much better sense of how comfortable you will feel during the shoot. Once you chose the photographer and decide on the type of wardrobe needed for the shoot, ask if you can e-mail your wardrobe selection prior to the session. This way, you will know if you are bringing the right clothes to the session.

Will you get black-and-white or color photos?
Years ago everyone began with black-and-white comps, because color was too expensive. Due to advances in technology and reduced reproduction costs, almost all comp cards created today are in color. You can begin with 50-100 comp cards and expect to pay anywhere from $70–$175.

How many photos will be taken?
Depending on how many different types of photos you are taking, you can expect anywhere from 36–200 images shot. However, the amount of photos taken is irrelevant. All you need is one great photo per image.

What will you receive after the shoot?
You can receive your images a number of ways. Some photographers will give you a CD with all of the photos taken after the session. Others might give you a password to view the shots on a website. You can ask if you will receive any printed photos free or if there is a fee for printed pictures. It is always best to see any photo you are considering using on your comp card printed on paper, as opposed to choosing it off of a CD or website.

Will the photographer select any photos?
It could be really helpful if the photographer would choose his or her top 5–

10 shots from the session. You might agree or disagree, but at least you will be getting one opinion from an industry professional.

Who owns the rights to the photos?
Legally, the images belong to the photographer. However, the photographer can only use your image for his/her promotional purposes. Your image can't be sold for profit without your permission.

How long will it take to see your photos?
It is a good idea to ask how long it will take before your photos will be available for you to see.

Will a fee be charged if you are not happy with the photos and need to reshoot?
Most photographers will tell you that as long as they did not make any technical mistakes—such as poor focus or lighting—they will charge the full fee to reshoot. Still, you should always ask, because I have heard of some photographers offering to reshoot either at no charge or for a discount if the model is not happy with the photos.

How should you handle the photographers' fees?
You should request (not demand) to pay a percentage of the photographer's fee up front, then pay the balance when everything that was agreed to is completed. Many photographers expect to be paid in full the day of the session. Just keep in mind that you always have a better chance of getting all of your photos delivered to you on time if the photographer has not been paid in full.

Try to get all agreements in writing and signed by the photographer. The agreement can be written in plain English. This is not a common practice, but it is worth trying.

Are there additional photography services?
Ask what the cost will be if the photographer does any retouching. Will the photographer recommend any printing companies to reproduce the photos? Are there any agents the photographer recommends you contact for acting and or modeling representation?

Hiring a Makeup Artist

You might wonder: "Do I really need to pay the extra money for a makeup artist? I could do the makeup myself." But, even if you are great at doing your own makeup, there is a big difference between the way makeup is applied for personal use and for the camera. (However, as I'll explain in the next chapter, it is also important for models to learn how to apply their own makeup.) Professional makeup artists know what the camera needs. They will also stay with you during the shoot, fix any hairs that have fallen out of place, and powder your face if it gets shiny under the lights. Makeup artists can help in other ways, too. I recently had a photo session for a new head shot. Even though I know how to do my own makeup, I hired a professional makeup artist. Not only did my face look better, but she noticed that I was leaning toward the camera slightly and was not sitting straight. This caused my head to look extremely thin and almost detached from my body. This slight adjustment made a big difference. Sometimes photographers can help spot problems while shooting, but they are concentrating on other aspects of the shot.

Fixing mistakes, such as out-of-place hairs or lint on one's clothes, can easily be performed with computer programs. However, it is better to catch and correct any problems during the session, rather then retouch the photos digitally after the shoot. It is a good idea to hire a makeup artist who is recommended by and regularly works with the photographer. A good makeup artist will always make you look better.

Sometimes the makeup artist can also serve as a "stylist." A stylist helps select the clothing or "wardrobe" and props for the shoot. For shoots with a large budget, a makeup artist is hired strictly to do makeup, and a stylist is hired to coordinate and purchase the wardrobe. If possible, discuss the shots with the makeup artist before the session. Show the makeup artist all the sample shots you will be doing. It is just as important for the makeup artist to understand the concept and feel of the shots as the photographer.

If the makeup artist is also helping with styling—wardrobe and props—ask if any special props or clothing are needed. If so, make a list of them.

If you have a unique skin tone and use special makeup, or can only use certain makeup because of allergies, always bring the makeup to your sessions. The makeup artist will apply it for you. Make sure you tell the makeup artist if you will be wearing contact lenses. He or she will be extra careful when applying makeup around your eyes.

Don't allow your skin to burn in the sun. Sunburn is never good for you, but especially not before a photo session. A young girl I know sat out in the sun for many hours just days before getting photos done for her composite sheet. When she got her pictures back, she noticed that her skin actually looked orange and red.

Before the Session
Make sure an iron is on the set, even if you have to bring your own. Wrinkled clothing makes a shot look unprofessional. Unless the clothes should be wrinkled to achieve a particular look, always have the wardrobe look neat and clean. Everything should be planned ahead of time so there are no major surprises on the day of the shoot.

After checking everything on your list, iron and hang all the wardrobe in a garment bag the night before a morning session. Place all props in a bag. Make sure you get a good night's sleep. Go over the list one more time in the morning. One of my very first jobs was working as an extra on a TV series. I was hired to be a waiter. I was so excited that I threw my wardrobe together that morning and went rushing off to the job. When I arrived on the set (which was a hotel in Washington, DC), I suddenly realized that I had forgotten to bring a very important part of my wardrobe: black pants. Fortunately I arrived twenty-five minutes before my call time. I literally begged every person connected with the hotel to lend me a pair of black pants. The few people who were kind enough to offer their trousers had waists that were either way too large or too small. I ran across the street to another hotel and paid a waiter just about everything I earned that day to buy his pants. Since then, I always go over my wardrobe list before leaving for a shoot.

Give yourself plenty of time to get to your session. Do not bring friends or relatives to the shoot (if you have already checked out the photographer). You don't want to be distracted by having your friends watch your session. This is a time you need to concentrate. Of course, this rule does not apply to the adult who brings a child model to a photo session. Sometimes the adult is asked to be present on the set to help the child relax, but other times the adult can be distracting and might be asked to wait in another room during the shoot. Once on the set, try to relax and enjoy the session. You will learn what to do on the set in the Go-See section of Chapter 8.

After the Session
Study the images. Ask other people in the industry for their opinions. If you haven't already, now would be a good time to begin contacting agents. Since agents will have different preferences about how to view photos, ask them how

they would like the images from your session delivered. You could create a few "mock" composite sheets to test out with industry professionals. Take four photos from the session and have them scanned and printed by a local store that has high-quality printers. Include your name, contact information and statistics (you will read more about this later in this chapter), and show these to agents for feedback. This will save you a lot of money. If the agent loves the photos, then use those images to print your new comp card. If the agent did not like the shots, then you only spent a few dollars creating them. See if any photos jump off the page. Before selecting the shots for your comp, make sure you really like them. Your pictures are representing you. In some cases you only get one chance to meet with an agent, art/creative director or photographer, so do not waste a good opportunity by showing poor-quality photographs. If the shots did not work, do not use them. Try to figure out what went wrong and shoot them again.

I do this exercise during my in-person workshops, and you can do this as well. When you are trying to decide on the image for your head shot and commercial photos, ask people who do not know you very well how you are perceived. What type of job do you have? Or if you are a student, are you smart, a troublemaker, the class clown, a bully or well liked at school. This will help tell you how you could be cast for projects.

This is what happens when you walk into a casting office. Before you even say hello, the casting director has already decided if you will be considered for the part. Everyone has a certain presence, and that is what you want to capture on your head shot. I asked people in and out of the business (who did not know much about me) how they viewed me. Nice guy, friendly, honest, warm, smart were some of the descriptions I would repeatedly hear. After learning that information, I knew what kind of feeling and image I wanted to project for my head shot (see photo).

Photo by Joe Henson

Shooting head shots and commercial photos can be hard. Just because you do a session, don't think that you will always get exactly what you need. Be prepared to go back and do things again. Maybe the expressions you wanted were not there. Perhaps the wardrobe did not quite fit the image desired. You might not have been able to relax during the session. Some photos do not work because of the photographer: the lighting is bad, the picture is out of focus or the camera angle is not complimentary to your face. If you like the way you look but not the overall photo, then you might need to find a new photographer. It is better to wait, figure out what is wrong, and try it again. It happens to everyone.

After choosing the photos for your comp, make sure you have at least two hard copies (or multiple backups on a CD, external hard drive or in the Cloud) of each photo you want to use. You always want extra copies in case something happens to the original. Don't depend on the photographer to keep backups of your images.

One quick comment about the photographer's name or photo credit. Some models put the photographer's name by the side of the photo on composite sheets. This is a courtesy to the photographer, but it is not necessary. If all of your shots were taken by one photographer, you might not want to list the photographer's name, because it will immediately show your lack of experience. If you have appeared in a lot of ads, you will have worked with many photographers and can list many different photographers' names. It is your choice, but one name on all the photos is a dead giveaway of inexperience.

Designing and Printing Your Composite Sheet

Every printing company has its own style and design for its composite sheets. Simply choose which format you think looks the best. You must decide how much of an investment you want to make. You don't need to have your first card printed by the most expensive printer. Hopefully, you will get some bookings and print a new card with a few actual ads within a year. One job could pay for all of your comps. If you are not willing to make the investment of creating a quality card, then you are not giving yourself a chance to see what you can do in this industry.

Agents will not pay for the model's comp card; that is our responsibility. *The Marcus Institute's Industry Information Directory* includes close to 20 printing companies that specialize in printing head shots and comp cards (see Chapter 13: Resources). You can visit their websites to view their work and get prices. Before deciding on a company, ask for samples of their work. It is important to physically see their products before making a final decision.

Just about every printer will ask you to upload a high-resolution digital image to their website. Find out what pixel count is preferred. The higher the number, the better the photo will look. Ask your photographer to save the image with the same pixel count as required by the printer. Make sure the printer knows where you want each photo placed on the comp card.

Ask how long it will take to complete your job. Clearly understand all of the costs involved. Some companies will charge additional setup, mailing and retouch fees if needed. It is a good idea to pay an additional fee to see a sample of your completed comp card before they are all printed. You might find a problem that can be easily fixed before you get your entire order printed. You should also ask about the price to reorder more copies at a later date.

How Many Comps Should You Order?
It depends on your situation. If you are just getting started in the business and not marketing yourself, then 50 comp cards should be plenty.

You will only be using the card when attending go-sees. If you are working with a number of agents in different markets, and sending out cards on your own, then make sure you have enough to last before you create a new card. Depending on how much marketing you will be doing, you might consider getting 100–150 cards printed.

When you first get your comps from the printer, save a few dozen in a special place for emergencies. You never want to tell a person requesting a comp that you just ran out. It looks unprofessional and you could lose a lot of money if it costs you a job. Order more when you see that you are low on comps.

Get quotes for ordering different amounts. You might be surprised how little difference there is between 100 and 200 comps. One of the big costs with composite sheets is the printer's setup time. Once a printer begins printing, you are only paying for extra paper.

The Ingredients of a Professional Composite Sheet
All comps should include:

1. Photos
2. Information about your size and appearance:

For a woman:	**For a man:**
height	height
bust	suit size
waist	neck/sleeve
hips	waist
dress size	inseam
shoes	shoes
eye color	eye color
hair color	hair color
hat size	hat size
glove size	glove size
ring size	ring size

3. Union affiliation: state whether you are a member of SAG-AFTRA, AEA or ACTRA.

4. Name, area code and phone number, and e-mail/website address, if you have one. You don't have to use your personal phone number. You can get a free www.google.com/voice number and have all calls forwarded to a designated phone. This keeps the world from getting your personal number. If you are only working with one agent, then your agent might prefer you only have his/her contact information on the comp.

5. Special qualities: for example, if appropriate, mention that you have excellent legs, hands, feet, or teeth.

6. Any sport or activity you are proficient in.

7. You may want to place the photographers' names on the comp, next to the photographs they took.

Composite Sheets for Children

If you are interested in getting your child or children in the business, you are probably wondering if a composite sheet or head shot is really needed. The best thing to do is ask the manager or agent you are working with or want to work with, and find out how they want to submit your child's photo. Different agents have different policies. Many agents require only a digital photo of a child under the age of three, since children's looks change so quickly. A photo that is three months old might not properly represent the child's current appearance. After the age of four (depending on how quickly the child's look changes), most agents will request a head shot. A composite sheet is only used when a child has very different and distinctive looks, and it might not be needed for very young children.

SIX
Makeup

Both men and women should learn how to apply their own makeup. At the very least, all actors and models should know how to put on base and powder. Most faces have slightly uneven shades of lightness and darkness. Putting on a base will smooth, darken, and even your skin tone. Imagine the base as a canvas for a painting. Once the base is applied, you can begin "painting," by applying other makeup on top of the base. The base will help cover up slight imperfections, and if needed will hide a five o'clock shadow. The powder helps take the shine off your face. This is extremely important when you are working under hot lights.

For many jobs, models are expected to do their own makeup. The better you are at putting on makeup, the better you will look in the shot. This skill will also help you at go-sees. You can cover up circles under your eyes, dry skin or other blemishes before a photo is taken. I had a go-see in February. The character was supposed to live in Southern California and spend a lot of time outside in the sun. I did not have much of a tan, but because I know how to apply makeup, I was able to put foundation over my hands, face, neck and ears and rouge on my cheeks to give me a sunburned, outdoorsy look. I really looked the part. Knowing how to apply makeup gives you a great advantage at go-sees and auditions.

When you work with a professional makeup artist, ask about the best products and tones for your face. If possible, get a basic demonstration of how to apply makeup. Watch the artist work on other models. Perhaps there is a school in your area that teaches makeup application. If you do not have contact with a professional makeup person, go to a cosmetics store and speak to a professional about products and application used for modeling or acting in front of a camera. These products are different from everyday makeup. If you have a unique skin tone and use special makeup, always bring it to the set, even if a makeup artist has been hired.

Basic List of Makeup and Other Items You Need to Bring to a Set

For women:

- Concealer for around eyes
- Current eye shadow
- Eyeliner
- Facial cleaner
- Good foundation
- Hair spray
- Light blush
- Lip gloss (variety of shades)
- Mascara
- Matte lipstick
- Nail polish (neutral colors)
- Nail polish remover
- Skin lotion
- Toner
- Translucent powder

For men:

- Base or foundation
- Blush
- Concealer for around eyes
- Gel for hair
- Hair spray
- Razor and shaving cream
- Skin lotion
- Translucent powder
- Vaseline (for lips)

Additional Items to Bring to a Shoot

You probably won't need to bring all of these items. Pick and choose the ones that are most relevant for you:

- Aspirin/Tylenol
- Black/brown reversible belt
- Bobby pins
- Brush
- Comb
- Compact mirror
- Cotton swabs—Cotton Balls
- Dental floss
- Deodorant
- Extra composite sheets
- Eye drops
- Hair ties
- Head bands
- If appropriate, extra stockings: white, black & blue
- Light snack (nonperishable)
- Lint brush
- Moisturizer
- Mouthwash
- Nail clippers/emery boards
- Name of photographer/street address
- Portfolio
- Reading material
- Shampoo
- Small emergency sewing kit/safety pins/extra buttons
- Small first aid kit
- Small towel
- Toothbrush
- Toothpaste
- Vouchers and booking information
- Ziploc bags for small items that could spill

SEVEN
Finding a Good Agent

An agent's job is to submit your photos to various industry professionals, send you on auditions and go-sees, give you the necessary information pertaining to a booking, and negotiate and collect fees when you are booked for a job.

Photographers, art/creative directors and the clients select models and actors for jobs. All you can ask of your agent is to be submitted. An agent who has worked with a photographer, casting director or art/creative director for many years might be asked to suggest or recommend a specific actor or model. If one of these industry professionals agrees with the suggestion, then that talent will get top priority and have his or her photos shown to the client or will be asked to attend the audition or go-see. The agent, however, does not select talent for jobs.

Quite often there is no way to know why one gets cast. Sometimes, the casting process seems entirely arbitrary. For example, I was once cast as a construction worker. I was very surprised because I do not see myself as having the construction worker look. After the shoot I asked the director why I got the job. He told me that at every construction site there is always one person who looks like he does not belong there. So, oddly enough, I got booked because I did not look right for the part.

Fees for Agents

Agents who specialize in print modeling generally take a 20 percent commission per booking. If you have an exclusive contract with an agent, you might be responsible for paying your agent a percentage of all of your bookings, including those you get on your own. Travel reimbursement (train or plane fare) is separate from the hourly fee and is not subject to commission.

Sometimes models get paid for the time they spend traveling to a job, when the shoot is in a distant location. Agents will take a commission from that fee. But, if a model is getting paid a fee for the miles they drive, then normally no percentage is taken by the agent. Agents collect a fee only when they obtain a booking for a model. The only exception to this rule is when a model decides to be on an agent's website or a different website the agent uses. I will discuss these in more detail in Chapter 8: How to Get Work.

Listings of Agents

There are many ways to find an agent. Some are very traditional methods; others require using your creativity and ingenuity. You can find over 400 agents from every state in the United States by visiting my website at www.howtoactandmodel.org. The *Call Sheet*, which is published by Backstage (www.backstage.com/resources) details hundreds of casting directors, talent agents, managers and production companies, mostly in the NY and LA markets. It also lists theaters, schools and film festivals. It is primarily used by actors, but some actors' agents also represent commercial models. You can also use www.auditionagency.com/agency_directory.htm to find agents. You will want to finish reading this chapter before contacting any agent. It is important to know how to prepare before a meeting, the right questions to ask and what types of answers you should be getting to make sure the agent is legit.

Contacting Agents

By using *The Marcus Institute's National Directory of SAG-AFTRA Offices* (for more information about this directory, see Chapter 13: Resources), you can find your nearest union office online and see the list of franchised agents who are signatories with SAG-AFTRA. This can be viewed even if you are not a union member. These agents have signed contracts with the union, agreeing to honor and abide by many rules and regulations. Many of these franchised agents also have commercial modeling divisions along with their TV and radio departments. Although this is a limited list, you can get a start in finding a good agent.

There is no guarantee that these agents are wonderful and trustworthy, but you will have a much better chance of finding good representation with franchised agents than by picking names blindly out of a large directory.

It is always best to visit the agent's website. Normally, the site clearly explains how new talent should contact the agency. If it says no phone calls, honor that request. A few agencies offer "open call." Open call is when an agent allows new people to come to his or her office and introduce themselves.

If the website requests talent to upload photos, then you should do that, but in addition to uploading your pictures, I have another suggestion. To make sure that your materials are seen by an agent, you might consider mailing a hard copy through the U.S. Postal Service. Make sure you have the agent's correct mailing address and that you have correctly spelled the agent's name. You don't need to spend extra money on a fancy envelope. A plain 9 x 12 envelope works fine when sending a head shot, comp card and cover letter. If you are only sending a cover letter and comp card, you can use a smaller envelope. Make sure your contact information is on your resume as well as on your comp card, so the agent knows how to contact you. You will also need to create a strong cover letter. If you have worked already, briefly describe your experiences. Do not address it "To Whom It May Concern." Your package will be viewed much more favorably when sent with the agent's name on the envelope and on your cover letter. This applies to all mailings.

Sample Cover Letter

Here is a sample cover letter. Keep it short and to the point.

Your name
(Head shot, so people see your face as they read your letter)
Union affiliation (SAG/AFTRA, if you are a member)
Phone number
e-mail address & Web address

Date
Jeremy Jen
c/o The Brooke Agency
6817 Nancy Way
San Diego, CA 91941

Dear Mr. Jen:

Enclosed is my newest head shot and composite sheet. I am a fresh face in this market (this is a great line—especially if you have never had a job) and would like to talk with you about representation for (choose the areas that are right for you) TV/radio commercials, feature films, TV shows and voice-over, promotional and commercial modeling work.

I look forward to hearing back from you at your earliest opportunity.

Best wishes,

Your name

Make Sure Your Materials Are Seen

To make sure your package is actually viewed by someone, you can also create a return letter and place it inside a prestamped envelope addressed back to you. Have the agency information in the return address so you know who the note is from. In the letter you could say:

> [ ] We have viewed your materials and would like you to contact us.
> [ ] We have viewed your materials and are not interested at this time.
>
> If you are not interested at this time, would you share some details about why and whether there are any other agencies in the area who you think might be a better fit for my look and talent?

No matter what the response is to your mailing, at least you will not be wondering if the agency received it and what they thought, and this will save you from having to contact an agent who might not want to hear from you.

It is so much easier to find agents today by simply searching online. When I first wanted to get into the business, I did not know the names of any agents. Nor did I know about any lists of agents that were available. I had to be creative. You might find these ideas helpful. First, I attended a number of plays and talked to the actors afterward. I told them how much I enjoyed their performance, and then asked them for the names of the best commercial agents in the area. I contacted the local Chamber of Commerce to get the names of the largest advertising agencies in the area. I called a few art/creative directors and asked them which agents they used when booking actors and models for ads. I also asked them for the names of a few photographers in the area. Then I contacted the photographers to find out which agents they used when booking models for commercial jobs.

In some areas, it can be difficult to find an agent. An actor I know was looking for a New York agent. He sent out his head shot, with copies of awards and reviews from plays he had appeared in (which included a wonderful review in *The New York Times*). He mailed his package to 160 agents, but he received only one response. However, that agent signed him, and he has landed some great film and TV roles. For print work as well as TV and film, you only need one great agent for your career to take off.

Make Sure the Agent Is Legitimate

Most agents are honest and hardworking people, but there are a few scam artists out there that you should be aware of.

There are some people who call themselves agents but actually make their living ripping off actors and models. They prey on people who make decisions based on their emotions instead of good sound judgment. Often, they will tell you that you have a lot of potential and that their guidance will make you a star. They might ask for up-front money. If that happens, walk out the door. With rare exceptions, the only time you will pay an agent any money aside from a percentage from a booking is if you are asked to be on a website. This is how agents promote their talent.

Legitimate agents make their money by getting a percentage of the bookings they get for the talent. Corrupt agents make money not by submitting actors and models and helping to get them booked, but instead by forcing talent to have photos taken by one photographer or by having them sign up for their class before they will offer representation. I understand why an agent would not want to represent people whose acting/modeling skills or photos are not where they need to be. The agent does not want to look bad by submitting people who are not ready. But a legitimate agent should not care where you study or who you shoot with, as long as you are ready to audition and work.

A few years ago I saw an ad in a Washington, DC, paper from a "New York" agent who was relocating and looking for actors and models. It felt like a scam to me, and I wanted to see firsthand how these thieves operate. I called and set up an interview with the "agent." I pretended that I had no experience and told him that I wanted to be a model. He told me that he rates everyone on a scale of one to five. If I was a five he would represent me. He told me I was a four. I told him how disappointed I was and began to leave. I knew he was not going to let me walk out the door. As I put my hand on the doorknob he said, "Aaron, you know what, you are a four but you are very close to being a five. In fact I know a great photographer who could turn you into a five. With the right pictures I could start sending you up to New York." What he failed to mention was that the "great" photographer was part of his company.

I should have gotten an Academy Award for the excitement I showed when I found out that I could become a five and be sent to New York. I told him that I had never been professionally photographed; still he was promising to send me to New York. No credible agent would risk his reputation by sending someone with no experience to the largest commercial modeling market in the world. I asked the agent, "What do I do next?" He whipped out a contract and said, "All you have to do is sign here." I very quickly glanced at the contract and noticed the cost of the photo shoot was $1,200. I told him I definitely wanted to do this but I would have to look the contract over at home and come back the next day. He put his hand on the contract and told me that "the contract does not leave this office." He also said that "a model's and agent's relationship is built on trust. If you can't trust your agent, then your agent will not be able to get work for you." I told him that I would have to call him back, and left. This guy was a sophisticated and manipulative con man.

To help you choose a reputable agent, I have put together a list of things to look for when interviewing with an unfamiliar agent:

- Make sure your appointment is scheduled during work hours.
- Always meet the agent at his or her office. Do not meet with an unfamiliar agent anywhere else.
- Look around the office. Are there copies of ads (tear sheets) the agency has booked for their models? If so, this is a good sign.
- Are the phones ringing? You want to see a busy office.
- Ask to see the head shots and comps (or view them online) of the actors and models the agent represents. Do they look good? You might want to request to see more photos of a few of the models whose ads are displayed in the office. Charlatans have been known to fool people by displaying ads of models they do not represent. If an agent is really working with a model, he or she should have the model's composite sheet or additional shots of the model on the agency website.
- Study the agent's website prior to your appointment. Look at the talent he or she represents.
- If you know any models who work with the agent, call them before your interview. Do they like the agent? Do they get work through the agent? Does the agent treat them well? Are they paid on time? (Generally modeling payments are made within 90 days.)
- Do you feel comfortable with the agent?
- Go to the website of the **Better Business Bureau** (www.bbb.org) to see if any complaints have been made against the agency. Having a few complaints doesn't necessarily mean the agency is bad.
- If the agent lies to you, makes outrageous promises or asks for money not normally paid to an agent, then keep looking. There are plenty of great, legitimate agents that you can find.

Signing with an Agent

Some commercial modeling agents ask models to sign exclusive contracts. If you sign an exclusive contract, you may normally only accept bookings from that agent. You may, however, be able to accept a booking from another agent if you obtain permission from your agent. If you are not signed with an agent, you can freelance and accept bookings from any agent. Agents in certain markets, like Los Angeles, require models and actors to sign exclusive contracts.

There are pros and cons to signing with an agent. On the positive side, you will have one person working very hard on your behalf. Life is simpler. When you are not available to work on certain days, you only need to notify one agent.

On the negative side, if your agent is not getting calls for the bulk of the projects in your area, work could be very slow for you. When you are first getting started, it might be better for you to sign with one agent and see how things go. If you are not happy with your representation, you can always change agents.

If you are just beginning, don't sign long-term agreements with an agent you are unfamiliar with. Typically, a franchised agent's initial contract (which will be mostly for acting jobs) can only last one year. If asked to sign, find out how many other actors and models in your "category" are already signed. Your category includes other talent who could be booked for the same job as you. There will always be other signed actors and models in your category, and it is not in your best interest to be one of 200 who could be submitted for the same job. However, if the best agent in your area does have a lot of talent in your category, then still consider signing with the agent. Have confidence in yourself. Become one of the top talent in that large list and be the actor or model who is submitted on projects regularly. It can take an agent six months or longer before submitting a new talent for auditions. Don't give up on an agent too quickly. Do everything you can to give the agent great materials. Stay in touch with the agent to let him or her know what new classes you are taking or what local plays you are working on. The important thing is to keep your face and name in the agent's thoughts. That is a great way to get remembered for new projects.

Before signing with an agent, make sure you understand everything in the contract. If you are not sure about something, show it to a lawyer. Be cautious. To help you research an agency or file a grievance, here are some helpful websites: **Internet Crime Complaint Center** (www.ic3.gov) and the **Federal Trade**

Commission (www.ftc.gov). Don't feel you have to avoid an agency just because a few negative complaints have been filed against them.

Getting an Agent's Attention

If you want to be represented by a particular agent, but you are having a difficult time making a connection, here is something you can try. Market yourself and book a job on your own, and ask the agent if he or she will handle the booking. Chances are the agent will be glad to represent you. It will be easily made money for the agent. The small percentage that you will lose will be well worth the connection you will have made. The first time I gave a booking to an agent, I actually made money because the agent negotiated a much higher fee than I could have.

Managers and Casting Directors

A manager is the person who provides counsel and helps guide every aspect of an actor's career. A manager works with a smaller group of people than an agent does, offering more personal attention. The manager gets paid by taking a percentage (approximately 15%) of any jobs the client books. The manager does not negotiate fees for the actor; that is the agent's job. If you just moved to a new area, the manager will help connect you with the right head shot photographer and acting classes. The manager will also find the perfect agent for you to work with. To learn more about managers and how you can find one, visit the **Talent Managers Association** at www.talentmanagers.org and the **National Conference of Personal Managers** http://ncopm.com.

A casting director is hired by a producer to find actors for a project. The casting director will break down the roles in the script (character's age, type, ethnicity, etc.) and send the details to agents and managers and sometimes post the details online. Then the industry professionals (or the actors) will submit their talent to the casting director in the hopes of getting an audition. If selected, the actor will audition (either in person or by uploading a home audition) with the casting director. Quite often casting directors will decide who will get the opportunity to audition solely based on the actors' head shots. That is why it is crucial to have an effective head shot. To make contact with many casting directors, visit **The Casting Society of America** at www.castingsociety.com.

EIGHT
How to Get Work

The best way to get work is to find an agent, or agents, who will submit you for projects.

Agency Websites
An agent either has a website or has the talent upload marketing materials (head shot/resume, commercial photos and reels) to another company's site. The only fee an agent collects from actors and models, aside from a percentage of the talent's bookings, is a fee to appear on the agency website. If the talent is using another company's website, then they will pay the other company and not the agent for that service. Yearly fees for appearing on an agent's website can range from $100 to $350. The fee for appearing on another company's site can range from $50 to $125. Being on the site allows your materials to be seen by many types of industry professionals. Agents can select and instantly e-mail the specific images that are desired for a project. Sometimes, talent can be booked directly from the website without having to attend an audition or go-see. It is difficult for an agent to promote and work with a talent who isn't willing to have materials online.

There is no guarantee of getting work, but having your marketing materials available online is a must and will greatly increase your chances of working.

Selling Yourself
Some people think that once an agency begins submitting them, all they need to do is wait by the phone. This is a dangerous way to run a business. You will get more work if you market yourself. Although many people e-mail JPEGs and resume attachments to industry professionals in order to get auditions and jobs, I believe it is better to send a hard copy through the mail along with a cover letter.

To help find contacts for TV commercials, radio spots and commercial modeling ads, I would suggest you visit a few advertising association websites.

See if there are any agencies near you. Many great ad agencies have chosen not to be affiliated with any association, so don't think that not being affiliated is a negative statement about an ad agency. Here are a few associations you can view:

American Association of Advertising Agencies at www.aaaa.org. To find agencies, go to the Agency Search link on the top of the site.
American Advertising Agencies at www.americanadagencies.com. Clicking on the link for a location will allow you to see the list of members there.

It's also helpful to send a short letter (with your head shot just below your name on the cover letter), post cards or new comps and/or head shots to the photographers and art/creative directors you have already worked with. This reminds them that you are still available for work. Some photographers will tell you it is a waste of time to send comps to them, because when they are ready to cast for a job, they will look at the agent's website or schedule a go-see. Yet I have gotten a number of jobs from photographers I had just sent a new comp or note to. I do not believe it was a coincidence. There is a photographer who I had never worked for, but I had heard good things about his work. Every time I put a new composite sheet together, I sent him one. This had been going on for three years. I never heard a word from him. Then one day, out of the clear blue, I got a phone call from his studio. He wanted to book me for a job. When I met him on the set, he told me that he always loved my comps but had never had a project that I was right for.

It is always helpful to keep your name and face in front of as many people as possible. After sending out your materials, wait about a week and send a follow-up e-mail. Make sure your head shot is embedded in your e-mail. Just ask if your materials arrived.

If you want to get work in different markets, having the ability to shoot clean-looking photos and home auditions is a must. If you live in Miami and want to be considered for bookings in Chicago, you can't easily fly to Chicago for an audition or even a request go-see (that is when a client specifically asks for a certain model to "audition"). Since the photographer and client need to see what you currently look like and/or be able to see your auditions, you can shoot the audition at home and upload it to the people at the ad agency or casting director. Some markets need to have the talent arrive in person, but it is always worth asking if you can submit your audition online.

If you are working with one agent or feel your phone number could change in the near future, list your agent's name and number on your materials. That way, you will always be reachable. Talent who can't be reached will not work. If you are working with a few agents or plan to market yourself, have your phone number, including the area code, on your comp and resume. Since you never know who will get your materials, you may prefer not to have your personal cell or home number listed. Instead, consider getting a Google Voice number from www.google.com/voice. This is a free phone number that allows you to forward calls made to that number to any phone you choose. Using Google Voice numbers is a good way to protect your privacy and know that you are receiving a business call. And if a message is left, you will receive it in text format.

Staying in Touch with Your Agent

You must check your phone, e-mails and/or text messages throughout the day. Agents will not try to get you work if you don't respond to their messages. Sometimes agents will call your phone if they have not heard back from you after sending you an e-mail or a text message. Keep the outgoing message on your phone short, and to the point. Sometimes agents won't wait for a long message to finish. If they are busy (which they normally are) and calling a number of talent, agents might hang up and move on to the next talent who they can connect with more easily. Don't have songs playing or long messages. Identify yourself at the beginning of your message, so the agent knows the right number has been called.

If possible, quickly mention a job you just had or when you are booked out in your message. That is good marketing and lets people know when you are and are not available.

After receiving a notice about a booking, audition or go-see, respond to the agent as soon as possible, even if it's to let him or her know you can't accept the job or attend the audition or go-see. Sometimes an agent only has a limited amount of people that he or she can send to a go-see or audition. If you are not free, give the agent an opportunity to send someone else. When agents spend large amounts of time trying to track down talent, that leaves them less time to promote them.

Portfolios

Years ago, models would bring a portfolio case filled with their photos to all go-sees. Even though it is rare that anyone requests to see portfolios today, still, you always want to have additional photos available just in case someone asks to see more pictures. Instead of purchasing a portfolio case, you can have your photos available on an iPad or with a phone app. You can download a phone app called Go See, and another one is called ModelFolio, available at http://modelfolioapp.com.

Working in Other Media

Although commercial modeling only involves print advertising, I recommend trying to work in as many media as possible: TV, film, radio, narrations, industrial films (also called corporate and educational films). These films are shot for government agencies, associations and businesses. All of these fields require the use of the same basic acting skills, so if work in one medium is slow, a different medium might be booming.

Go-See

What is a go-see? A go-see is an audition for print jobs such as magazine, billboard, poster or newspaper ads and for Internet sites. It generally takes place at a photographer's studio or casting office. After you get the notice about a go-see, there are some important things you want to ask and/or tell your agent:

- Who or what is the ad for? You need to make sure you are comfortable supporting and promoting the campaign. If not, thank your agent and tell him/her why you are not going to attend the go-see.
- Make sure you are available for both the go-see and the shoot date.
- Ask your agent what character is being cast so that you can look the part.

When you arrive, there should be a sign-in sheet and a model form to fill out. Models write their names and sometimes their agents' names on the sign-in sheet. This plain piece of paper lets everyone know who is next in line to have his or her photo taken. At some go-sees, models are asked to write their names on small white boards or pieces of paper. The board or paper is held under the model's chin for the first photo taken. This easily identifies the model. Since you never know exactly when your name will be called off the list, do not sign in until you are completely—physically and mentally—ready to have your photo taken.

Sample model form

    (NAME OF PHOTOGRAPHER OR CASTING STUDIO)
    DATE:
    NAME:_____PHONE:_____
    AGENCY: _____ PHONE:_____
    HEIGHT: _____ SIZE:_____
    WAIST:_____ HIPS: _____
    SHIRT: _____ HAT:_____
    WEIGHT:_____ BUST:_____
    SHOES: _____ SUIT: _____
    INSEAM: _____ GLOVES:_____
    AGE:_____ HAIR: _____
    EYES: _____
    ARE YOU AVAILABLE FOR TESTING? YES _____ NO _____
    THANK YOU
    STUDIO USE:
    COMMENTS ON MODEL!

The model form asks for:

- Your name
- Agent's name
- Sizes
- Phone numbers, etc.

    This information helps the stylist purchase the correct size clothing for the model selected for the job. It also lets the casting people know which agent to contact. Fill it out and hand it to the photographer or an assistant, along with your composite sheet. Make sure your agent's name and phone number are on your comp. If a home address is requested, I leave that blank. I don't like sharing that personal information with people I don't know. And, you have no idea who might see this information when your card is discarded after the go-see. Another reason not to list your home address is if you traveled to another city to attend a go-see. You might not want people to know that you live out of town. Sometimes that can keep a model from getting the booking, because some people are uncomfortable hiring out-of-town models. If an address is required, perhaps you could use your agent's address.

If you are attending a go-see or a TV commercial audition for, let's say, an insurance company, you might be asked to write down any previous jobs you have had with those types of businesses. Talent might not be hired if they worked on a project for a competitor. I have saved a list of these types of jobs I have previously done and bring the list with me to every audition and go-see. This easily allows me to write them down if requested.

Layout
After filling out the model form, see if there is a layout. A layout is a vague image of the ad, which is used as a guide by the photographer, stylist and art director. It might give you specific information about the character being cast. You can see what the character looks like. Is the person wearing glasses? What are the attitudes and expressions?

If a layout is available, use a mirror and try to make yourself look just like the character in the layout. Perhaps you need a little makeup or your hair needs to be combed again. You should also get yourself mentally prepared. Think of the message of the ad. What kind of emotions are being looked for? Think of the situations from your past or present that will allow you to actually feel the emotions needed for the shot. When you are ready, sign in. When it is your turn, a photographer or an assistant photographer will take the photo.

Always ask what type of character is being looked for. Sometimes it is hard to fully understand the layout, or perhaps your interpretation of the ad might be different from the photographer's. Concepts can change and the layout may not represent the real image wanted. The assistant photographer might not know much about the ad, but it's worth asking.

Right before the shot is taken, you will be asked to stand on a mark on the floor (usually a piece of tape) or sit on a stool. Having everyone stand or sit in one spot means that the lighting can stay the same for everyone and makes focusing the camera easier for the photographer. Now is the time to use all of the techniques you have practiced. To help you concentrate on feeling the appropriate emotions, try looking at the floor or toward a wall. Once you feel the emotions, look straight into the lens or wherever you have been asked to look. If the layout shows the character looking away, look away. Try to copy the layout as closely as possible. If you need a moment to create that look, ask for it.

If you did not give the look you wanted, ask if they will take another photo. Sometimes they say yes; sometimes they say no. I once went to a go-see for an ad for a new drug being given to cancer patients. I was supposed to look like

Don't Get Locked In. Get A Second Opinion.

Upgrading your information system is no job for amateurs. Systems vendors are experts in selling products, not solving problems. Accountants who crunch health care numbers may know zero about health care. Before you're locked in to costly off-the-shelf solutions, get a second opinion from ASPEN's Health Information Systems (HIS) specialists. Beside a complete mastery of current automation technology, they have years of hands-on experience in the health care field. Best of all, they'll be working for you. And only you.

Look Before You Leap

Customized Solutions

No two health care providers will answer those questions in exactly the same way because no two operations are identical. That is why the ASPEN HIS team begins with an exhaustive analysis of your operation and its unique needs. Only then are they ready to recommend customized systems options that are both affordable today and adaptable to expansion tomorrow. But hardware and software alone do not make a system.

The People Factor

Any system is only as good as the people who use it. In an age of laptop, bedside and notebook terminals, real-time processing of health care information is passing into the hands of your medical staff. The ASPEN team offers programs to educate your doctors and nurses, pharma-

Layout-Shandwick USA

a person with cancer. I tried to look sick, had the photo taken and left. As I was getting on the elevator, it hit me that I gave a cold or flu kind of sick look, and not a more serious diseased expression. I felt a little uncomfortable, but I went back and asked if I could try a different look. They said yes, and I got cast for the job. I might have gotten the job even if I hadn't gone back, but I felt much better knowing that I gave it my best try.

Photo by Evan Cohen-Me imitating the layout image

Photographers have go-sees so they can see what you currently look like and how closely you resemble the person in the layout. Your composite sheet is viewed to see your range of looks. Normally, digital photos are taken, but on occasion the go-see will be videotaped.

After your shot is taken, ask if the photographer wants a second composite sheet for his or her files. It is rare that they want to keep your comp card, but it is worth asking. So, always have extra comp cards with you.

A go-see should be viewed as a job. It is a good way to introduce yourself to a photographer and an art/creative director. Never turn down a go-see. You never know how important one might be.

I once had an 8:00 a.m. audition in Washington, DC, and a 12:30 p.m. go-see in New York. I rushed around like a mad man. There was a train delay and I knew I would be late to the go-see. I called my agent and she suggested I still go. When I arrived about 20 minutes late, I realized why: There was a line that went down two flights of stairs, out the door and around the block. I waited in line for two hours. Some people decided to leave. But after all I had been through to get there, there was no way in the world I was going to walk out of line and go back home. I did have some doubts, though. There were a lot of beautiful men and women in line, and I wondered, "What in the world am I doing here? Does my agent have any idea what I look like?" I was feeling intimidated when I heard people talking about their latest movie roles and their recent TV bookings. I finally made it upstairs, where the photographer was asking the models, on videotape, what they had done recently. Most people discussed their latest bookings. I knew the photographer must have been bored to death listening to hundreds of people talk about their latest jobs. I wanted to say something that was relevant to the shoot, but would also make me stand out. Since this was an outdoors shot, I decided to tell him that what I did most recently was go on a camping trip with my family. As it turned out, among the hundreds and hundreds of people who attended the go-see, I got the booking and was flown to Hawaii for the shoot.

I have gone to go-sees where I knew I was not right for the part and did not get the job. However, I was booked by the same photographer for a different job sometime later because the photographer remembered me.

There are a million reasons why people are and are not chosen for a job. Although it is difficult, try not to spend much time and energy wondering why you were not chosen. All you can do is give the look you are trying to achieve. The final results are out of your hands. If you did not give the look you wanted, try to figure out why, and how you can achieve that emotion for future go-sees or bookings.

Along with getting bookings, you should also use go-sees as an educational tool and a learning experience. They offer opportunities to introduce yourself to new people and to remind people you have already worked with that you are still around.

How to take a better photo
Some models show up to a go-see wearing anything they happen to fall into that particular day. They assume all photographers, casting directors, art/creative directors and clients can use their imagination to see if you are right for the part. Don't count on it. You should look the part that is being cast. (This philosophy can change for certain acting auditions. Some casting directors feel insulted if you arrive at an audition wearing too much wardrobe. A good casting director can tell if you are right for the part purely by your acting skills.) For go-sees, I prefer not to leave decisions up to people's imaginations. I like to hit them over the head with a look so they immediately think, "Yes, that person is perfect for the job."

If the client makes the final casting decision, then you are certainly better off dressing the part. Clients are not in the advertising business and might not be able to see beyond the photo. Even if the photographer, art/creative director or casting director can envision someone looking a certain way, they may not be able or want to fight to get the model they want approved by the client. If they are looking for a businessperson, look like a businessperson.

You never know if they are going to take a close-up shot or a long shot of your whole body, so wear the whole suit, not a suit jacket and a pair of shorts.

Know your face. Be aware if one side of your face looks better in photos. Once you have that information, you can always turn your face slightly toward the camera to show your best side. If your nose looks large in a profile shot (that means sideways), never turn completely sideways in front of the camera. You can "cheat to the camera" by turning your face a little toward the camera. This technique will make your nose look shorter. You can see how different your face can look by experimenting with different expressions and angles with a digital camera or cell phone.

Conflicts
After you appear in an ad for a certain product, all competing products are considered conflicts. For example, Coca-Cola would be considered a conflict if your Pepsi ad is still running.

Before going to a go-see, ask your agent about the product. If there is a conflict, make sure your agent is aware of it. Sometimes agents are told not to send anyone to the go-see who has done an ad for a competing product within a certain time period. Exclusivity fees are sometimes paid to the model so that the model will not work for a competitor. Once I did a job for a chain of hotels. For one year I could not do ads for hotels that were considered to be competitors. Before accepting other hotel jobs, my agent had to get permission from the advertising agency that paid me the exclusivity fee. If no exclusivity fee is paid, models may work for anyone who hires them. If there are any questions about a possible conflict, inform your agent.

Castings
A typical go-see in New York could easily draw 50 or more models auditioning for the same job. The selection process can be handled a number of different ways. Sometimes the photographer decides who gets cast for the job. Other times the photographer and/or art/creative director will pick three (or more) people and list them as their first, second and third choices. Phone calls go out to their agents to put the three models on hold. That means the models must hold the shooting date for that project. The model can't accept other bookings on that date without first clearing it with the agent. The first agent to put you on hold has the right of first refusal. That means if you get another job offer for the same date you are holding, you must have your agent call the photographer or art/creative director who initially put you on hold and get you either booked or released. That allows the photographer or art/creative director to hire you before anyone else for that date. You can only accept the second offer after being released from the first job.

Sometimes models are put on hold because a number of people—as many as seven or eight—might be involved in the casting process. Putting a number of people on hold gives everyone extra time to decide exactly who they want for the job.

Sometimes it is the client who makes the final decision after getting input from the art/creative director and/or the photographer.

Information You'll Need After Accepting a Booking
- Date of the shoot
- Name and type of product
- Name and phone number of the contact person
- Name of the ad agency
- Name of the photographer

- Time and length of the shoot
- Location of the shoot
- Type of character desired
- Type of wardrobe needed
- Whether they will have a makeup artist on the set
- Billing and usage information (I will explain more about usage and billing later.)
- Fees

Agent Submittance
Another way to get booked, which does not involve a go-see, is through agent submittance. An ad agency or photographer might call an agent and request a specific look. The agent will e-mail JPEGs of models who fit that description.

Agent's Website
Another way of getting booked for a job is from the agent's website. Because of the time and expense involved in holding casting sessions, sometimes models are booked directly or requested to attend a go-see right from the agent's website. Unlike a composite sheet, photos on a website can be easily updated.

Direct Bookings
Models usually get bookings through agents, but they can also be hired directly by photographers or art/creative directors. There are pros and cons to being booked directly for a job. On the positive side, when models are booked directly, they do not have to pay an agent any commission. And talking directly with the photographer or art/creative director means there is less chance of any confusion about the particulars of the job (time, location, wardrobe, etc.). However, a model who is booked without an agent has little recourse if he or she is not paid. Legal action is always a possibility; however, the model must determine if the time and money invested in the legal proceedings is worthwhile.

Before taking any direct bookings, make sure you have a firm understanding of the business end of modeling. It is easy to lose money because of lack of information. Your agent can negotiate and get the proper fees, and he or she knows if any bonuses are applicable to the job.

If you take a direct booking, make sure whoever is being billed for the job (the photographer, advertising agency or client) signs a voucher or a similar document after the session. A voucher is a bill and contract, which is discussed in more detail in Chapter 9: How to Work as a Professional Model. When booking through an agent, the model does not have to submit invoices to the client or act as a bill collector if the payment is late.

Don't underestimate the work involved in bill collecting. I once had a job with a client from Europe. I was paid within 90 days for the travel days (getting to and from the shoot), but I was not paid the bonus fee or for the actual shooting day. I spoke with my agent and was told that the photographer was having some financial problems. Another month went by. My agent told me that the photographer would start paying in monthly installments. The photographer paid his first month's installment, but no check arrived for the next month. I asked my agent what should be done. She said that she had worked with the photographer for many years and believed that he would eventually pay. My agent made many, many calls and sent dozens of letters. It took one year, but I was eventually paid in full. Agents generally have a working history with photographers and advertising agencies. They know when to push to have a check sent and when to wait.

Occasionally, a model is unable to collect the fee for a job. This should be a rare experience. Only once have I not been paid for a job, and that was because the client went bankrupt. Sometimes a company that goes bankrupt opens up again under a different name. If that happens, do not work for them again until you have been paid in full for your previous work.

Neither photographers nor ad agencies nor clients want to have the reputation of not paying their bills. If an agent is not paid, he or she can and should refuse to allow any of his or her models to do any future work with that client.

Good agents are knowledgeable and selective about who their models work with. If you get a call from someone wanting to book you directly and you have any doubts about their legitimacy or intent, you should definitely refer that person to your agent. Let your agent make sure the person is really in the advertising industry.

NINE
How to Work as a Professional Model

What Is Expected of a Professional Model?
Make sure you look like you. Photographers have told me horror stories of models who are cast from their composite sheets or website photos, and then show up on the set looking like different people. That is one of the problems that can occur with using computer programs to remove scars or wrinkles from your photos. Your pictures must be up to date and accurately represent your appearance. It is fine to have your photos retouched to cover up wrinkles, blemishes, or minor scars as long as you have the skills to cover them up with makeup and look exactly like your photos when on a set or at a casting. I have known models who were fired when they arrived at the photographer's studio because they had misrepresented their looks. You may actually hurt your chances of being cast by hiding your distinctive characteristics.

Depending on how quickly your physical appearance changes, adult composite sheets should generally be updated every two years. Some children might need them changed more frequently. The best rule to follow is that you should get new photos made when your old ones no longer look like you. If you undergo any physical changes, such as extreme hair style or color changes or weight gain or loss, you must notify your agent. This is especially true if you made a physical change after attending a go-see where you were booked for the job.

I learned a very valuable but painful lesson about a change of appearance. I went to a go-see for a national ad campaign. A week after the go-see, I accepted a two-week booking for the U.S. Navy. I had to get a haircut for the job—not a buzz cut, but a pretty conservative look. The following week I was told I had gotten the national ad. I took the train to New York, went to the studio and met the photographer. He asked me if I had cut my hair. I told him yes. He looked at my hair again and told me that it was too short for the ad. They found someone else that morning to replace me. I felt awful about losing the job and very embarrassed about the situation. I should have told my agent that I had cut my hair before going to the shoot. I will never make that mistake again.

Be Responsible

Once you agree to attend a go-see, you must show up. If for any reason you can't attend, tell your agent. The client is expecting to see the requested models and a number of others. The client is spending a lot of money and wants to have a lot of choices in order to decide who is perfect for the job. If the client or photographer requested to see you, then it will create tension between the client, photographer, and your agent if you do not show up. This will not help your relationship with your agent.

Never show up late to a job or a go-see. It makes you and your agent look bad. If it happens enough times, your agent will not submit you and photographers will not request you.

Being late for a job sets up an uncomfortable atmosphere. I was at a shoot where the model I was to work with was not on time. Everyone was waiting: the photographer, the client, the stylist, the art director, the copywriter, the assistant photographer and the account executive. Not only did the model cause the project to cost thousands of dollars more, but he also created a very tense atmosphere on the set. Neither the photographer nor I could experiment and try out creative ideas. There was a limited budget and a limited amount of time for shooting. Because so much time was lost waiting for the model, everything was rushed. The photographer had to go with a very straightforward traditional shot. Everyone was unhappy. Models can be held financially responsible for money lost because they are late.

I have heard models say, "What is the big deal about showing up a little late? Most of the time you have to sit and wait for the photographer anyway." That can be true. Many times you sit and wait for the photographer, but it is your responsibility to show up on time. Don't forget, you are getting paid extremely well to sit and wait. Showing up late makes everyone in the modeling profession look bad.

Give yourself plenty of time to get to a job. Allow extra time in case you get lost, hit traffic or have parking problems. If you happen to show up very early, go inside and let someone know you have arrived. Ask where you can hang up your wardrobe and find out where you should wait. Leave the photographer alone. He or she might be prepared to shoot right away or could be incredibly stressed out because of a technical problem. You will be told when the photographer is ready. If you are running late for a job, call your agent to inform him or her when you will arrive on the set and to find out if you still have the booking.

Sometimes being late is simply out of your control. Once I had two morning go-sees in New York. I gave myself plenty of time to attend both castings.

My train was an hour late and still I had time for both go-sees. After the first go-see, I took the subway to get to the second one. But someone had pulled the emergency brake on one of the subway cars, and I had to wait a half hour for the next train. The 10-minute trip turned into a 45-minute adventure. The second casting ended at 12:00 and it was 12:15 by the time I arrived. My point is that sometimes you have no control over your arrival time. Always give yourself extra time. Even with bad luck, you still may be able to keep your appointments.

You Were Hired to Model
It is very important to remember why you are on the set. It is because you were chosen to be a model in an ad. The set is not the place to try and sell any products or services you might also be involved with. If someone asks you about any other jobs you might have, you need not shy away from answering, but do not walk on the set with samples of cosmetics or other products that you are trying to sell. The people who have hired you do not want to deal with anything except getting a great photo with you. This also holds true with discussing family problems or scheduling difficulties. Focus on your modeling work.

Wardrobe
Part of your high hourly fee goes toward being prepared with the proper wardrobe. Double-check the wardrobe list you got from your agent or stylist to make sure you have everything. Don't skimp on bringing clothes. Sometimes you feel more like a moving company than a model, because of all the things you are hauling to the shoot. If you bring more clothes, the photographer has more choices. Even if a stylist is bringing some clothing, you still might want to bring wardrobe that is appropriate for the shoot. That can translate into a better-looking shot, which will help you get future jobs.

If a model only brings one shirt, one tie and one suit for a business shot, the photographer will not have any options. If the colors or styles are not right for the shot, then you are cheating yourself out of a possible great tear sheet and an enjoyable experience with the photographer. The photographer can try to get another suit, which will take a lot of time, or just go with what the model brought and not be very happy about the look.

I was on a shoot where the other model brought one shirt and one tie that were identical to mine. Fortunately, I brought a few extra pieces of wardrobe. The photographer would not have been very happy to have two models wearing the same clothes. Bring a wide variety of clothing so wardrobe is never an issue at a shoot.

Don't forget all the accessories that go along with the wardrobe. Always dress from head to toe. If you are asked to look like a businessperson, don't forget a watch. If you are to be a husband or wife, don't forget a wedding ring. Bring as many accessories as possible. And don't be surprised if, after you lug two garment bags of wardrobe into the studio, the photographer says that what you are wearing is just perfect. It happens often.

Unless specifically requested, you should avoid clothing that is white, red or black—these colors generally do not photograph well. This is true for black-and-white as well as color photos. Think about undergarments as well. Don't wear a white or off-white blouse and a red or black bra, or light-colored pants and black or red underwear. Wear white or off-white undergarments.

How to get wardrobe you do not own
If you do not own the wardrobe you've been asked to bring to a shoot, there are five things you can do:

1. Ask your agent if the photographer or stylist can supply the wardrobe.

2. Borrow the items from friends or relatives.

3. Purchase and keep the wardrobe.

4. Purchase the clothing from a consignment shop, then, if desired, resell it back to the store.

5. Ask a store manager if clothes can be borrowed for a shoot and returned after the session. In return, the store may get a name credit in the ad. Before offering the name credit idea to the store manager, get an agreement in writing from someone at the ad agency.

Food and wardrobe do not mix
If you take a lunch break during a shoot, make sure you don't spill any food or drinks on the wardrobe. The best thing to do is change your clothes. If that is not possible, find something to put on top of the wardrobe—perhaps an apron or a large towel. Be careful about wrinkling the wardrobe or doing anything to it that changes its original appearance. Just use some common sense.

Think before you speak
If you think the wardrobe chosen for you looks ridiculous, don't go around

saying, "What idiot picked out this garbage?" You were cast to look a certain way. You may not understand the concept of the ad or where or how it is being marketed. Someone invested a lot of time trying to figure out exactly how you should be dressed.

When to Put On Makeup
Unless you are told otherwise, do not put on makeup or put anything in your hair before arriving for a shoot. If the look is not what the photographer or art director wants, then a lot of time will be wasted in removing it.

You or the makeup artist will put on your makeup after the photographer or stylist selects your wardrobe and describes the kind of makeup he or she wants. Generally you will be dressed in your wardrobe before putting on makeup. This helps prevent smearing the makeup and staining the clothes.

On the Set
Stay in position. When you first walk onto the set, you will be told where to stand. The photographer will then look through the camera to see if the shot is framed correctly and if the lighting looks right. It is important to stay in one position, because if you move after the lighting is set, the shot might not look right. If you get tired being in one position, just ask the photographer for a break. Before moving, make sure there is a piece of tape or something on the floor marking your position.

Not all shots are done with the model in one position. Standing still could be inappropriate for certain shots.

Do not touch the props
Sometimes the set is filled with props. Don't play with the props. Positioning is crucial to the shot; if something gets moved even a few inches, it could make the difference between the ad looking real or staged. If an important prop is broken, the shoot might have to stop. Sometimes you need to have a prop moved in order to get in a certain position. If you notice a prop move while shooting, tell the photographer. It might not matter, but the information could be helpful.

You might be asked to hold a prop, especially if the item is the selling point of the ad. If you are using a prop, be careful with it.

Getting information about the ad
Before the shoot begins, make sure you have studied and understand the layout of the ad. Ask the art/creative director and/or photographer about

the kind of look, feeling and expression they want. If you are unsure about the ad's message, ask questions. It is crucial that you understand the ad and how it needs to be delivered. Without this information, you will be lost. The camera becomes your worst enemy. It will pick up the vacancy and uncertainty in your eyes. Think of ways to get the needed expressions.

This is where your acting training is very helpful. It is your responsibility to know how to deliver the look needed to make the shot perfect. Once you feel ready, just relax, create, and have a good time.

Getting conflicting information about the ad
The photographer is the one who generally supplies the model with information about the ad. But you may be confused if you get conflicting suggestions and comments from the photographer, art/creative director and even the client. In this situation, talk to the photographer privately. Tell the photographer about the conflicting messages and ask what you should do. The photographer might be completely unaware that other people were giving you different ideas about the shot.

Sometimes you are working with people who have big egos and are used to having their way. The client is spending a lot of money, so it is essential that everyone is pleased with the photo session. Art directors make their living by having things look a certain way. Photographers get rehired because their photos look great. Everyone has a lot at stake. Everyone needs to be heard, but generally it is the photographer who should be listened to. Most of the time the photographer is the link between the client, art/creative director and the model.

Never Discuss Fees

Never discuss fees with the other models, photographers, ad agency people or the client while you are working. Now is the time to concentrate on your work. It is your agent's job to deal with money. All discussions about fees should have been ironed out prior to the shoot. Two models working on the same set may get different fees due to their experience or longer travel time getting to the job. I've seen models get so involved in arguments that they were not able to concentrate on their work. Fees are a private matter between you and your agent. If you absolutely have to talk about fees, wait until after the session is completed.

Do Not Discuss Upgrades While Working

An upgrade is given to a model when his or her ad is placed in a high-exposure format. For example, billboard ads receive more exposure than ads running in a newspaper, and they are therefore considered upgrades. Appearing on a billboard can closely identify you with a product, which could prevent you from doing an ad for a competitor even years after the ad ran. Because of the overexposure you might lose work in areas where the billboards are located. An upgrade could mean thousands of additional dollars.

Let Your Agent Renegotiate Fees

Renegotiating fees is not your job. Let your agent work for his or her percentage. It is easy to be paranoid and think everyone is trying to cheat you. Sometimes what seems like an effort to rip you off is actually a mistake due to lack of communication. Once I was in a situation where my agent told me my ad would appear in a newspaper only. But on the set I heard that it was also going to be used on billboards. I finished the shoot. Before I signed the voucher, I called my agent to tell her about the change in usage. She spoke with the photographer, and I simply wrote the new information on the voucher. It was taken care of very easily. If I hadn't done a good job, the client might not have liked the finished product and scrapped the entire billboard idea, or the client could have kept the billboard idea and reshot it with a different model. Be professional, let your agent handle negotiations and just concentrate on your work.

The Voucher

When the shoot is over, you will be asked to sign a voucher (see a sample voucher on page 72). A voucher is a bill and a contract. It must be signed by the model and the person who will be billed for the job (that means the person who is paying). Always bring a few vouchers to each session. If you were booked directly for the job, an agent's voucher can be used. Scratch out the agent's name and put your name, address and phone number on the voucher. Each agent has his or her own voucher, which should contain the following information:

- Name of model agency
- Name of model
- Date job was done
- Hours of job

- Hourly fee
- Name of photographer
- Who gets billed for the job (the photographer or ad agency)
- Explanation of usage for the ad—e.g., billboard, point of purchase (a display ad in a store to promote the sale of a product), brochure, newspaper, poster, Internet, packages, etc.
- Time length of usage (typically beginning after the photo is published, not after the session date)
- Name of the product

Many vouchers have three color-coded copies. Sometimes the voucher is a single sheet and you need to make a few copies and give them to those involved in the shoot. The model, agent and person to be billed each get one copy. Keep your copy in a convenient and safe place. File your vouchers in chronological order so that you can easily see if any payments are overdue. For example, I did a job in 2013, then in 2015 I noticed the ad running in *People* magazine. I checked my records for 2013 and found the shoot date. Knowing the date made it easy to find a voucher that was two years old. The voucher showed a 12-month usage agreement. Since it ran past the 12 months and I could produce our original agreement (with the voucher), my agent was able to collect another payment for the ad. Models often lose money because of sloppy handling of their vouchers.

Sample Voucher

Computing the time for the voucher
When a model gets a confirmed booking, he or she will be told the hours of the shoot. Models can also be booked by the day or days. If your session goes longer than expected, your agent may have you bill in 15-minute increments (some to the next half hour). That means if you were booked for a three-hour shoot and it lasted three hours and 20 minutes, then you would charge for a three-and-one-half-hour session. Always ask your agent how you should handle things if the session runs longer than expected.

Here is a simple chart that shows you the quarter-hourly fees in relation to hourly fees. You should copy this and bring it with you on all shoots. This chart will make it easy to figure out the full amount of money owed to you as you write it in the voucher.

If you are making:
- $250 an hour, then you are being paid $62.50 every 15 minutes.
- $200 an hour, then you are being paid $50.00 every 15 minutes.
- $150 an hour, then you are being paid $37.50 every 15 minutes.
- $125 an hour, then you are being paid $31.25 every 15 minutes.
- $100 an hour, then you are being paid $25.00 every 15 minutes.

It is not a common practice, but if you are asked to change the finish time of a shoot by a few minutes in order to lower the cost of the session, there are a few things you can do:

- Insist on being paid for the time worked.
- Check with your agent before agreeing to the request.
- Say they must negotiate directly with your agent.

Once, I was working on a national ad campaign. The job was supposed to be a 2-plus-1 (a two-hour booking with a one-hour "hold"). That means the model must leave an additional hour open in case the shoot takes more than two hours to complete. However, this job took more than five hours. There were many delays because the client, art director, and copywriter were not able to agree on many things. We shot past 5:30 p.m., which is considered overtime according to my New York agent. When we were finished, the photographer, whom I have worked with many times, said, "The advertising agency will go crazy when they get the bill." I told the photographer if it would make it easier for him, I would forget about the overtime, and he could just pay me straight time. The photographer told me that I should get paid for my work and that it was not my fault we went into overtime. I mentioned it to my agent, and she was very upset with me. She told me that it was her job to negotiate. That is why she is getting 20 percent commission on my jobs. I do not offer reductions anymore without first clearing it with my agent.

The Model Release

After the session, you might be asked to sign a model release form. Signing this document means that you release your rights to the usage, design or overall image of the photograph. Read the model release carefully. It always says the photograph can be used in "any or all media," and for "any purpose whatsoever," or words to that effect. In the sample adult model release form I have printed those words in bold. Never sign it without scratching out the words "any or all media" and "for any other purpose whatsoever." Next, you should write in exactly how the ad will be used. For example, "in newspaper only," "brochure only," etc. Then initial it and sign it. By signing the model release without any changes, you are giving the ad agency permission to use the ad on TV, billboards and point-of-purchase ads or in any form of advertising, without paying you additional fees. On the next page is a sample adult model release:

ADULT MODEL RELEASE

In consideration of my engagement as a model, and for other good and valuable consideration herein acknowledged as received, upon the terms hereinafter stated, I hereby grant _____, his legal representatives and assigns, those for whom _____ is acting, and those acting with his authority and permission, the absolute right and permission to copyright and use, reuse and publish, and republish photographic portraits or pictures of me or in which I may be included, in whole or in part, or composite or distorted in character or form, without restriction as to changes or alterations, from time to time, in conjunction with my own or a fictitious name, or reproductions thereof in color or otherwise **made through any media** at his studios or elsewhere for art, advertising, trade, or **any other purpose whatsoever**. I also consent to the use of any printed matter in conjunction therewith. I hereby waive any right that I may have to inspect or approve the finished product or products or the advertising copy or printed matter that may be used in connection therewith or the use to which it may be applied. I hereby release, discharge and agree to save harmless _____, his legal representatives or assigns, and all persons acting under his permission or authority or those for whom he is acting, from any liability by virtue of any blurring, distortion, alteration, optical illusion, or use in composite form, whether intentional or otherwise, that may occur or be produced in the taking of said picture or in any subsequent processing thereof, as well as any publication thereof even though it may subject me to ridicule, scandal, reproach, scorn and indignity. I hereby warrant that I am of full age and have every right to contract in my own name in the above regard. I state further that I have read the above authorization, release and agreement, prior to its execution, and that I am fully familiar with the contents thereof.

Name:_____
Witness: _____
Address:_____
Date: _____

A release form for minors has the same information as for adults. The only difference is an additional section for the parent or guardian to sign the document.

Do not sign anything you do not understand, even if other people are doing it. Just tell the photographer that some things are unclear and your agent likes to read everything you are asked to sign. Some agents request that the model release form be sent to them before their model signs it.

If the photographer gives you a hard time about making some changes, just blame it on your agent. Ask the photographer to talk with your agent about the wording of the release, and follow your agent's advice.

Asking for a Tear Sheet
After the voucher and model release forms are signed, ask the art director if you can get a copy of the ad after it is completed. If the art director is not on the set, then try to make arrangements with the photographer. This is an essential part of the modeling business; you need new tear sheets to put together a new composite sheet or update your website pictures. It can be harder to get the tear sheet than the booking. You must be persistent but not obnoxious. Sometimes the art director or photographer will ask for your e-mail address and offer to send you a copy when things are completed, but they are very busy, and most of the time they will forget to send you a JPEG. So, always ask when the ad will be completed. Then ask if you can call or e-mail at that time to remind them about getting a copy. If you are not able to obtain the ad through the photographer or art director, then find it yourself. If it is running in a magazine, buy one and make a copy of the ad. If it is running as a poster in a store, contact the store and ask if they will give you a copy.

Information Needed from Every Job
Before leaving the set or location, make sure you have the following information recorded for yourself in a record book or saved in a spreadsheet:

- Date of job
- Hours worked
- Location of shoot
- Name of agent who booked you the job
- Photographer: name, address, phone number, e-mail, website
- Advertising agency: name, address, phone number, website
- Art director: name, address, phone number, e-mail
- Creative Director: name, address, phone number, e-mail
- Makeup artist: name, address, phone number, e-mail, website
- Stylist or prop person: name, address, phone number, e-mail, website

- Name of product (or job number)
- Type of character you portrayed
- Who to contact to get a tear sheet, and when the ad will be completed
- Notes about any unusual circumstances

Always remember, you want to present yourself as an experienced and professional model. Think about the long term. You are building relationships along the way. Every negative experience could hurt your chances of working. Every positive experience could mean more work in the future.

The Work after the Work
After the job, make sure you do the following:

1. Contact your agent to report the hours you worked. This immediately starts the billing process.

2. Personally deliver, mail or e-mail the agent's copy of the voucher that same day.

3. Make a note in your calendar of when you should contact the photographer or art/creative director requesting a tear sheet.

4. Create a message in your calendar 90 days after the job to make sure you have been paid. (The main reason the model has to wait so long for payment is because the model is the last person to get paid. The client pays the advertising agency, the advertising agency pays the photographer, the photographer pays the agent, and the agent pays the model. Sometimes the client is billed directly by the agent, in which case the model might get paid sooner. Even if the photographer is being billed for the job, he or she normally will not pay the agent until he or she is paid.)

5. Record and file all the important information concerning the job in a book or spreadsheet (date, name of agent, photographer, art director, etc.).

6. Keep a list of your mileage and any expenses that were job related. They could be tax deductible.

7. Send a note (make sure your photo is in the note) to the photographer and art/creative director to say that you enjoyed working with him/her.

8. Send a note to the agent thanking him/her for submitting you for this job.

Keep All of Your Vouchers Together

If payment is not received within 90 days, call or send a note to your agent. Never call anyone but your agent concerning an overdue bill. Give your agent all of the relevant information. Remember, your agent could be working with hundreds of models. The more information you provide, the quicker your agent can find out about a delayed payment.

Keep another list of when you get paid. Write "paid in full" on your voucher and date it. When someone sends you a tear sheet, send a thank you note.

Turning Down Jobs

There are times when your ethics or other considerations make it appropriate for you to decline a booking, but think very carefully before turning down a job.

Personal reasons

If you do not want to be associated with a certain product, don't accept the booking. I got a call from an art director about doing a job dealing with child abuse. It sounded like a very powerful and well-thought-out campaign. The message was that even regular-looking people—your friendly, helpful, next-door-neighbor types—could be child abusers. I had mixed feelings about the ad. I liked the concept, and thought it would be helpful to get that kind of information out to people. But I turned it down because I did not want to be associated with being a child abuser. I would not want my children or their friends to see me in that type of ad. I was also concerned about the possibility of losing work because of the connection with that type of character.

Doing a cigarette ad can be a difficult decision for some people. If you don't want to support cigarettes but are offered $12,000 to do an ad, it can be a tough choice. You could dislike the product but still decide to accept the booking. I knew a model who hated cigarettes but did a national cigarette campaign and donated most of the proceeds to the American Cancer Society. If you are offered a job advertising a product you do not wish to be associated with, seriously consider turning it down. Your affiliation with that product could haunt you for years.

Financial reasons

You might get a call to do a job, but the client can only pay $50 an hour instead of your normal $75 or $100 per hour. Some models automatically refuse jobs when they are offered a lower-than-normal hourly fee. Taking a job at a lower fee could make it more difficult to get your regular fee for future jobs.

Before making a decision, find out if the shot would be good for your portfolio. Maybe you need that "relationship" shot, or that "mom" photo or that "upscale" look. You might not earn much for the session, but the photo might get you a lot more work in the future. Are the photographer and art/creative director new contacts for you? If so, you might consider it a way of getting paid to introduce yourself to them. Also, you never know how long a shoot might last. I've been booked for a 1-plus-1 but the shoot has lasted three to four hours. And you never know who you might meet on a set. I met a model at a low-paying job who introduced me to an agent in another market I was unfamiliar with. I contacted the new agent and have been working with her for years. When I was just getting started in the business, I actually lost money on a job because of my agent's fees and transportation costs. I viewed it as a long-term investment. I knew that I would do a great job and if a future project came up that I was right for, I would be requested.

Sometimes models are hired as "extras" on a shoot. They are considered extras because their faces are not clearly seen in the shot, or because they are in the background. There is no specific fee established for extra work. Instead of an hourly fee, generally a flat rate is paid. The fees paid to the model can vary from $50 to $500 for the shoot. If you are asked to do extra work, you should seriously consider taking the job. Sometimes people get upgraded from an extra to a principal. Also, it gives you the opportunity to learn more about photo sessions, meet photographers and art directors, and network with other models.

One other reason you might want to turn a job down is if the ad is going to run in perpetuity. Sometimes clients want to be able to use an ad forever. There can be an additional bonus given to the model in this situation, but you should really think about this before agreeing to do the job. I was recently offered a job for an insurance company that would have paid $2,000. That is great, but they wanted to use the ad forever. The problem is that I could lose work and not be able to accept any jobs for a competitor throughout my career. There is a lot of modeling work in the insurance, health care, fast food and pharmaceutical industries, to name a few, and you might find that you will lose money in the long term if you have an ad running in perpetuity. So, I turned the job down.

I am not saying you should always refuse to do these types of jobs that will run forever, but before accepting or rejecting a booking, get the necessary information, think about what is best for you and then decide.

Two Agents—Two Bookings—Same Day

If you freelance with different agents and are booked for a job through agent X and another job comes in from agent Y for the same day, what do you do? Normally you would turn the second job down because you are already booked. But what if the first job is a three-hour booking that would pay hundreds of dollars, and the second job is a national ad campaign that would pay thousands of dollars?

The best approach in this situation is to be honest. Explain the situation to agent X, and ask if the shooting date or perhaps the times could be changed to accommodate both jobs. If not, ask agent X if it is possible to get you released from the first booking. Quite often the agents are understanding and can work things out to help you get the more lucrative job.

Keep in mind what you are asking agent X to do. He or she will have to explain to the client why you are no longer available and then spend more time finding a replacement and making sure the client is happy with the other choice. The agent could lose his or her commission if the client decides to get a model from a different agency.

If the agent cannot get you out of the smaller job, keep your commitment and decline the national ad. I have heard stories of models lying to their agents in order to keep more lucrative jobs. They accepted both jobs, then called in sick to the less profitable jobs. One agent told me about a model who was in that situation and simply did not show up for the smaller job.

Lying to an agent or not showing up for a job is a bad way of doing business. Agents will not represent people they cannot trust or rely on. In this industry, as in any industry, you must think about the long term. Don't do things that will sever a relationship with an agent with whom you work regularly. You may lose money by taking the smaller job, but it's worth a lot more to have an agent who trusts and respects your word and integrity.

When to Call an Agent

Always ask agents about their phone call policy. Find out if they want you to call periodically or send e-mails, postcards or letters to stay in touch. Also, find out how often they want you to reach out to them. Staying in touch is a good way to remind the agent that you are still around. Describe what you have worked on lately (theater, TV commercials, radio, classes, etc.). Listing recent projects is a good way to let the agent know that you are marketable. Do not try to stay in contact with an agent by walking into his or her office and beginning to discuss world events.

Unless you have something urgent to discuss, like a job-related problem, set up an appointment. This way the agent can give you his or her undivided attention. It is very important to have a good line of communication.

When You Are Unavailable for Work

If you are working with one agent, make sure the agent knows when you are unavailable for work. Because of last-minute calls about bookings, it is important that your agent knows your schedule. If you are working with a number of agents and will be unavailable for three or more days because of a booking or vacation or for any other reason, make sure they have the dates.

While on vacation, try and check your cell phone for messages or e-mails daily. It is important to get away from work, but you are the only one running your business. If calls come in, you are the only one who can handle them. You could lose a great booking by not checking messages. It also makes things hard for your agent who might be desperately trying to reach you.

If you are requested for a job, your agent has to get back to the photographer or art/creative director to say that he or she can't reach you. If it is a last minute job, your agent might get bombarded with phone calls from the photographer or art/creative director throughout the day as they scramble around trying to quickly put together a shoot.

How to Speak to an Agent When Work Is Slow

Do not call or stop into an agent's office demanding to know why he or she has not gotten you any work. That approach is never in your best interest. If you are not getting much work, there are better ways to approach an agent.

If your agent is submitting you to potential clients and you are still not getting any work, set up an appointment and talk with your agent. Make sure you are being considered for the right jobs. Ask if you need to change your photos. Ask your agent for some concrete suggestions on what you can do to get more work. Remember, it is in the agent's best interest for you to book jobs. That is how the agent makes a living.

Additional Modeling Fees

On top of the hourly or daily fee, additional monies are paid for certain high-exposure usages, such as:

- Billboards
- Point of purchase
- Displays
- Posters
- Packages
- Exclusivity
- Internet
- Side of a bus
- Usage longer than 12 or 24 months

In addition, some agencies charge an overtime fee if the booking is on a holiday or weekend or outside of the 9-to-5:30 working day.

Sometimes there are special rates for travel days, full-day bookings, prep time and the wearing of lingerie and transparent apparel. Prep time is the time needed for special preparation before a photo session. Once I was cast to be a Nostradamus type, and the makeup artist needed three hours to put my makeup on and 45 minutes to take the makeup off. Sometimes models are paid half the normal hourly fee for prep time.

Photo by Donna Marie Bailey

TEN
Auditioning

When you have a head shot and a comp card, know how to work in front of a still camera and have created a great resume, then find an agent. Your next step might be going from print ads to extra work and from there to TV commercials, and from those to small parts in TV shows and films. One of my early experiences with acting was getting booked for a modeling job and having the company want me to be in its TV commercial as well. Although I view commercial modeling as acting without words, still, there are some differences between commercial modeling and acting. For example, learning how to make other people's words sound conversational takes different skills from what is needed in commercial modeling. And, knowing how to prepare and audition for acting jobs is more complicated than attending a go-see. So, to help you branch out into the acting world, if that's something you want to do, I will share with you some strategies and techniques that will help prepare you to get acting jobs as well.

Preparing for the Audition
When you are first notified about an audition, there are a few pieces of information you need to get right away:

1. The audition and shoot dates—If you are not available for the shoot date, let your agent know. It might be worthwhile to audition anyway, because the shoot dates could change.

2. The type of project you are auditioning for—Is it a film, TV show or commercial? Make sure you are comfortable being associated with the project.

TV Audition
If you are auditioning for a TV show, make sure you watch the show. Know the names and relationships of the characters. Become very familiar with the style and pacing of the dialogue—is it fast-paced, or do people take their time delivering their lines? Is the show a drama or comedy? This information will help you tremendously during the audition.

Film Audition

If you are auditioning for a film, get the name of the director. To better understand the director's style, watch his or her movies. You can easily find the listings on IMDB—Internet Movie Data Base—www.imdb.com. After learning the names of the films, do a search on YouTube—www.youtube.com—to watch clips of the projects. This will give you a much better sense of how the director likes to see actors work.

Radio and TV Commercial Audition

If you are auditioning for a radio or TV spot, read the copy (the words in the commercial) for all of the characters, including the directions (if included). Make sure you understand all of the words and that you can pronounce them correctly. You can learn what pacing you need for the copy by timing your read. Your read should end at 28–29 seconds in a 30-second spot. The additional time allows for any additional information that needs to be added at the end of the commercial.

Don't make the mistake that many actors make when auditioning for commercials. It is not our job to sell. Our job is to tell a story. Don't just say the words—feel them. When you think and feel the part, your energy will be captured by the camera and grab people's attention.

To help bring the audience into your world, think of a key word or two that helps give you a reason to say your first scripted word. Then, start the first part of the first scripted word away from the camera and finish the word into the camera. Here is an example. The scripted copy is "This coffee maker is so easy to use." The word *Wow* could be your key word that gives you a reason to say your initial scripted word (*This*). Hear the word *Wow* in your head or say it very softly away from the camera, and then say the first two letters of your first word (*Th*) away from the camera, and finish the *is* directly into the lens. Have someone shoot you doing this, with a camera or even just a cell phone. You can try saying the first scripted word directly into the lens and then try it with my suggestion. When you start the conversation away from the lens and then quickly engage the camera, it is as if you are thinking of something to say and then talking to friends. This makes the friends (audience) feel like they are being engaged in your conversation. It also gives the audience the feeling that you are bringing them into your world. This is a powerful technique, and you will see a big difference when working this way.

If you can't memorize all of the copy for the TV spot, then at least memorize the first and last lines. You want to say both of those lines directly into the lens of the camera.

Physical Auditioning Techniques

Don't hold the copy or sides (the words in a TV/radio spot or the short portion of the script that is read during an audition) down by your waist. When you look at the words, the camera will only see the top of your head. Try holding the copy closer to your eye level, but to the side, so it does not block your face. I like holding my thumb on the line I am about to read and then sliding my thumb down to the next line. This helps keep my eyes in the correct place on the page. I also view three words at a time, say them to the reader (or camera), then grab the next three words and continue reading this way. Using this technique will help you look and sound more conversational.

Where Is Your Eye Line?

For TV commercials: Look into the camera (you can look away—but normally you will return to looking into the lens of the camera).

For film/TV: Read to the reader (who is normally by the side of the camera) or other actor. (Exceptions: If auditioning to be a news reporter or news anchor, then you are most likely going to read into the camera.)

Studying the Sides

Begin reading the sides as if reading a grocery list. No acting at all! This allows you to feel comfortable with the words, and it keeps you from getting stuck on reading the lines in a specific way. Once you decide how you want to play the character, begin making specific acting choices and use your skills to make the character come alive.

You always want the people watching your audition to believe they are there in the scene with you. To help make that happen, imagine a life before the scene begins and after the scene ends. If there is a direction in the sides that says your character is running late for a meeting, then bring that type of energy into the first words of the scene. Always extend the end of the scene by two to three seconds, or longer. You don't want to say your last word and abruptly end your audition. That jolts people who are watching the audition and takes them out of the scene too quickly. If the character you are talking with walks out of the room, follow him or her with your eyes. Have some type of reaction to what just took place. This will help finalize the scene.

Make sure you read everyone's lines in the script before the audition. Quite often you will find that it is another person's lines that will tell you a lot about your character.

Figure out who the scene is about. If the scene is not about you, don't try to make your character the star. There are many talented actors who make a great living by playing supporting roles.

Look in the sides to see if there is a change to the character. If so, what is the change and where in the script does it happen? Then make sure you show the change in your audition.

The Five W's
As you are working on the sides or copy, always use the five W's:

Who are you talking to? Make it specific. Know your relationship with the character. You will speak differently to your father than to your ex-boyfriend.

What are you talking about? What is happening in this conversation?

Where is the scene taking place? Your voice needs to match the location of the scene. Are you on a busy street corner or on the couch in your living room?

When is this conversation happening? Are you talking at 3:00 a.m. or 1:00 p.m.? Your voice and body language should properly connect with the time this scene is taking place.

Why are you having this conversation? The reason for the talk will also inform the way you act.

Memorizing Scripts
There are many ways to memorize a script. There is no one right answer for everyone. Try out many methods and pick the one or a combination of techniques that work best for you:

1. Write out all of your lines by hand on a piece of paper four to five times. This really helps plant the words in your head.

2. Try singing your lines. Just like a song that you easily memorize, adding a melody to your sides is a great way to memorize lines. I find this especially helpful if there are technical words in the sides.

3. Figure out how many lines you need to memorize in the script. Divide that number by the number of days you have before the shoot (but plan on having everything memorized by three days prior to the shoot date). The first day, start at the beginning of the script and memorize your minimum amount of lines. Every day after that, review the lines from the beginning of the script and continue, memorizing the minimum for that day. For example, if you have to work on 4 pages each day, on the first day you memorize pages 1–4. On the second day, you work on the first 4 pages, and then memorize pages 5–8, and so on. This repetition will help imprint the lines into your brain.

4. Search and download a rehearsal app. There are a number of programs that will help you memorize lines. You can find a great app in the Resources section of my website at www.howtoactandmodel.org.

5. Run the lines with another actor. Practice the lines in different locations. This makes it easier to adapt to saying your lines in different settings—like on the set.

6. I have never used this method, but an actor told me how helpful it was for him to record his lines and have them play over and over again as he slept.

Nervousness

If you find yourself getting nervous before auditions or on sets, don't feel bad. It happens to many people, even well-known actors. I have worked on over 1,200 jobs and sometimes I get very nervous. Instead of trying to get rid of your nervousness, use it to your advantage. I like it when I am nervous; it puts more energy in my read. The trick is in learning how to harness that energy and use it in a positive way.

Mental exercise

I am not a negative person. However, I am pretty realistic. One of the tricks that helps me with nervousness is to think, "Why should I be nervous? I probably won't book this job anyway." When there are many people auditioning for one role, there is a really slim chance that I will get cast. I also know from experience that there are many reasons for booking and not booking a job. Getting cast is completely out of my hands. That is why I don't bother pressuring myself with "trying to get booked." My audition is the only thing I have control over.

My three audition goals
I have three goals when attending auditions. My number one goal is to have a good time. I really want to enjoy myself during those few minutes with the casting director. My second goal is to learn from the experience. Sometimes, I feel like I did exactly what I had prepared and that I had a good day at work. Other times, if the audition did not go as well, I will try to figure out what happened, think about how I could have done things differently and then use that information for my next audition. My third goal—last on my list—is booking the job. If it happens, it is like icing on the cake. I find that thinking this way takes a lot of pressure off of me during my auditions. There are others who build up their confidence by thinking, "Of course I am going to book the job." If that works for you, use it. I tried that strategy once and did not find it helpful. Going into an audition thinking that you must book the job will likely add to your nervousness. And, everyone in the room who is watching your audition will feel your tension. Understanding the realities of the audition process can help calm you down.

Physical exercises
Here are some physical exercises you can perform to help harness your nervous energy:
1. Place one hand over your heart and the other over your belly button. Close your eyes and take a deep breath. Let it out slowly. You will still feel the energy, but it will be much more contained.
2. Shake out your nervousness by jumping up and down with an imaginary rope.

I would not suggest you perform these exercises in front of anyone; instead, do them before you get into the casting office or in the bathroom prior to your audition.

Secrets to Auditioning
You have already succeeded just by getting the audition. Hundreds and sometimes thousands of actors are submitted for one role on a project. Every casting director and project is different, but sometimes only 25–40 people are invited to audition. So, getting the audition is really an amazing accomplishment.

The casting office
When you walk into the casting office, treat everyone with respect. I have heard some actors get nasty and begin complaining to the person sitting at the front desk. That person might be the casting director's son or daughter, or perhaps he or she will be starting a new casting company soon. Having a bad attitude can prevent you from being invited back. Plus, it is no way to treat others.

When you walk into the casting room, always have the attitude, "If I book the job, that's great, and if I don't book the job, that's fine too; I will book another one." People want to see an actor exude confidence. They want to hire someone they can trust and who they want around on a set. So, even if you are shaking inside, use your acting skills to portray someone who is confident and upbeat.

Don't immediately extend your arm to shake people's hands. Some people don't feel comfortable doing that. You can simply say hello, and if they want to shake your hand, just follow their lead.

Questions for the casting director
Before you slate (I will explain what that means shortly), this is the time to ask the casting director any questions you might have. For example, if you are not sure of the meaning or pronunciation of a word, or about your character's relationship with another character, always ask. Any question that will make your audition better is expected and appreciated by casting directors. But don't ask how they want you to read the sides—that is your job to figure out. If you are taking the character in a direction that does not seem right to the casting director, he or she will give you some information and ask you to read again.

Slating
Sometimes, but not always, actors are asked to "slate" during their auditions. Slating enables casting directors and others to easily identify you before watching your audition. It also gives them a taste of your personality. You could be asked to give different information for every slate. Sometimes, you are asked to say your height, weight, agent, where you live, the role you are reading for, etc. This should always be said directly into the lens of the camera.

There are two different philosophies with slating. Some people feel it is better to slate in character. That way, the casting director and director believe you *are* that character. The other way is to slate as yourself. I suggest slating as if you are meeting someone at a party. Say the information requested in a nice, warm and friendly way. After the slate is done, look slightly away from the camera, take a beat, get into character and start the audition. That is the technique I use. This allows people to see that I am an actor who can make specific character decisions. The director might feel more comfortable hiring someone who can act, rather than someone who simply resembles the character.

Making mistakes
We are all human. We all make mistakes. Auditioning is not like the Olympics. Points are not deducted if you drop a word or two. What is important is that you physically look right for the part, bring life to the character and read in a conversational way. If mistakes happen, what is crucial is how you handle the error. If it is at the beginning, just say that you would like to start over. If it is toward the end, ask if you can read it again. No matter what the casting director's response is, accept it. Always remember, people are not looking for the "perfect" read. They understand that it is okay to make a mistake.

If you have another idea for how to read your lines, simply ask the casting director if you can read it a different way. Just make sure there really is a change in your delivery.

Apologizing
No matter how poorly you felt you did at the audition, never apologize. Never say "I am sorry," lower your head and walk out of the studio. Always leave your audition as if you gave the greatest performance of a lifetime. A negative attitude can change the way people perceive your audition. A positive and confident attitude can also boost people's perceptions of your read. There have been times when I thought I bombed the audition, yet I left the room with confidence and booked the job. Always leave an audition with a positive attitude.

Nothing personal
I have learned that not booking a job is not a statement about me. Casting is, essentially, a business decision; it's nothing personal. Whether the job happens for me or not, I still have people in my life who care about and love me. And, not getting the role is not even a statement about my audition. The casting director might have loved it but thought I was too tall or too short, too thin or not thin enough. Maybe he or she is looking for someone to play the father of a teenage actor, and I don't look enough like the actor. There are a million reasons why you might or might not book the job. It really is nothing personal, so don't take it personally.

I view every audition like making a bank deposit. Sometimes it can take a lot of "deposits" before the money substantially grows. I have auditioned and not booked the job but have had the casting director ask me to read for other roles. I have even been booked for jobs without having to audition, because the casting director had seen me audition numerous times and campaigned for me to be cast.

On-Camera Home Auditions

It is crucial that all actors and models have the ability to shoot photos and auditions remotely, either at home or by paying someone for this service. There are certain markets where talent is often booked in this way. In the long run, it is more economical and easier to shoot auditions if you own your own equipment. Paying someone else to shoot your audition does have some benefits, but it can get costly and sometimes getting a last-minute appointment can be difficult.

In my home office, one light sits on a desk, another is on the floor and a third light attaches to the screen, which is permanently attached to the wall. The light clipped to the screen helps keep shadows from appearing on the screen behind me. The desk and floor lights, one on each side of my face, keep my eyes looking alive and my face evenly lit. (There is more information about lights in the equipment list below.) My laptop, which I use as my camera and mic, is placed on a box that sits on a pulled-out drawer from a filing cabinet (see image on page 92).

Once the audition is completed, I do some minor editing and then send it online to the agent or casting director.

Equipment for Home On-Camera Auditions

Here is a list of the basic equipment you will need and specific techniques to use to make your on-camera auditions look and sound great:

Camera: This does not have to costs thousands of dollars. You can find a good digital camera that also shoots high-quality videos in the $300 range. I use my Mac laptop to shoot all of my auditions. The auditions look clean and clear.

Cell phone: The majority of casting directors I have interviewed do not like auditions shot on a cell phone. I also find it much easier and quicker to edit the audition if it is shot with a camera or on

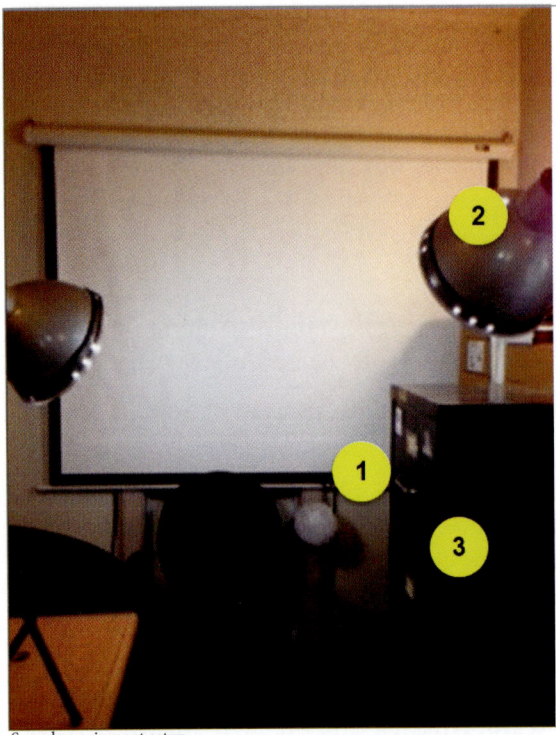

1. Back light to keep the shadows off the wall

2. Two lights on the side of my face to keep my eyes clear and my face sharp

3. Cabinet drawer that gets pulled out that holds my laptop

Sample equipment setup

a laptop. If you get a last-minute audition and you are not at home, then you can use a cell phone. You should ask, but most casting directors will want the audition shot in a horizontal not vertical position. To keep the cell phone from shaking, you will want to purchase a cell phone tripod and adapter. You will also want to download a good video editing app.

Lights: I use three lights for my auditions. You will need light stands for two lights (the third light is clipped to the bottom of the screen) and a diffuser for each light and maybe a reflector. The diffusers, which cover the bulbs, will help soften the light on your face. If you need additional light on your face, a reflector is useful. Don't use regular bulbs. Make sure the bulbs you use are specifically made for the light stands you have purchased. You want to use light bulbs that don't create much heat, otherwise you will find yourself sweating during your auditions. Always have a few spare bulbs handy in case one dies during an audition.

Microphone: You can use either a shotgun or lavalier microphone (I use the internal mic that is built into my Mac). The lavalier mic attaches to your wardrobe. You can try running the wire underneath your clothing, to hide it a bit, but it is fine if the mic is seen during the audition.

Tripod: A tripod is essential to hold the camera steady during your audition.

Screens: If you have a clean and smooth white wall with nothing on it, then perhaps that can be a substitute for a screen. Or, you could purchase a collapsible background—5 x 7 white, blue or green screen. Another option is a plain pull-down that attaches to a wall.

Buying the equipment
Visit your local camera store. Let people know that you will be using the equipment for home auditions. See what equipment they recommend. Perhaps they can offer you competitive prices—similar to the ones found online.

Programs for editing videos
You can find great editing programs and a comprehensive list of the necessary equipment and software needed for your home auditions by visiting the Store page on my website at www.howtoactandmodel.org and ordering the Shooting Auditions from Home Online Workshop. You will also find software and product information on the Resources page of my website.

Voice-over software
A great voice-over program that is free is listed on the Resources page of my website at www.howtoactandmodel.org.

Microphones for audio recordings
An earbuds-mic combination can be used for a basic voice-over audition, but the sound won't be great. You can find the mic I use and really like on the Resources page of my website at www.howtoactandmodel.org.

How to Position Yourself During Your Audition
Sit or stand; the decision is yours to make. If you need to slate, you will look directly into the lens of the camera. For the actual audition, you always want to address the "reader" (the person who is reading all of the other character's

lines). The reader should be slightly to the left or right of the camera lens. I prefer looking camera left (my right), but it is up to you. If, for some reason, the reader can't be in that spot, you should still be looking and speaking slightly to the side of the camera. You want the reader to say the lines loudly enough that the casting director can hear them, but not so loudly that they overpower your voice.

Some people prefer to have a reader who is a trained actor. That can be helpful but it is not absolutely necessary. If you get a last-minute audition and you don't have a group of actors who help each other with home auditions, then you have to use whoever is available. A nonactor can read the lines in a plain way, with little to no emotion. You just want to make sure that there is nothing done by the reader that stands out in a negative way. Having a nonactor as a reader allows me to read my lines exactly how I want, without being taken into a different direction by the other actor's character choices. The trick to having an effective audition while reading with a nonactor is to make strong decisions about your character and the other characters you are reading with. Hear the lines from the reader, just the way you imagined them to sound, and then react accordingly.

Don't Over Shoot

We have the luxury of shooting multiple takes when auditioning from home. But, be careful that you don't shoot it so many times that the final version has you looking and sounding tired and bored. This can happen easily when shooting at home. Your audition does not have to be "perfect." If your read was great but you missed a word or two, save that version. If you can say the words properly in another take or two, then delete the older version. If not, send in the version that sounds and feels the best, even if there are a few minor mistakes.

Uploading Your Audition

Never post or upload an audition on social media. The sides or copy must never be seen by anyone. Sometimes actors are asked to sign an NDA (Non-Disclosure Agreement) before auditioning. This is a legal document saying that you will not discuss or share the audition information with others. Take this legal document very seriously. I have heard of agents and casting directors who stopped working with talent who posted their auditions online.

If you are sending a radio spot audition, typically your MP3 file will be small enough to attach to your email. However, even short video auditions are normally way too large to send this way. There are a number of companies that allow you to upload large documents. Some are free; others ask for a nominal annual fee.

You will find some great programs that allow you to both reduce the size of your video (some companies won't allow huge files uploaded to their sites) and upload them, on the Resources page of my website at www.howtoactandmodel.org.

Better to Audition with a Casting Director
Even if I can audition from home, I will travel three or four hours to read with a good casting director. My audition will always be better when reading live. And, in person, the casting director will share more information about the project, and give directions and suggestions based on what the director wants to see. So, if you have the option, I would recommend that you audition live. If you simply can't travel, then audition from home.

ELEVEN
The Realities of Being a Full-Time Actor and Model

Being Self-Employed
Although actors and models are submitted for jobs by agents, they are considered to be self-employed. There are many benefits to being your own boss. For example, you decide how hard you want to work. I know many people who act and model part-time, get a few bookings a year, and are extremely happy with their acting and modeling situation. Others pursue acting and modeling as their full-time occupation and can earn $20,000 to $250,000 or more annually.

SAG-AFTRA and AEA withhold money from each paycheck for taxes and offer health and pension benefits to those who qualify. Models and non-union actors do not get any health or pension benefits or money withheld for their taxes. At this time there is no union for models. Hopefully, in the near future a union will be formed that will offer similar benefits to models.

If taxes are not being withheld from your paycheck, you should talk to an accountant to make sure you are saving enough money to pay your taxes and have money for retirement.

Is Acting and Commercial Modeling for You?
I truly love my work, but there are aspects about the business that I don't always like. It can be demoralizing, frustrating, frightening and stressful. It can also be exhilarating, wonderful and an extremely rewarding profession. As in any job, there are no guarantees, but the more knowledgeable and skilled you are, and the harder you work, the greater the chances are of achieving the success you desire.

When I began, I decided not to have any specific goals for my first year. I just wanted to experience the work and the lifestyle to see how it felt. I am not saying you should not have goals, but before goals are set, first find out if acting and modeling is something you really enjoy. Make sure that an uncertain income is something you and perhaps your spouse and family can handle. Most important, make sure you love the work.

If acting and modeling interests you, try it. It is always sad for me to hear people say they wished they had tried acting and modeling, but now they simply can't. Whether you are successful or not, if you try, you will not have to look back and wonder how far you could have gone in the field. Even if you only get one booking in your entire life, it will be well worth the effort. Being professionally photographed and seeing yourself in an ad or in a TV commercial or film is an incredible experience—one that will last you a lifetime.

Start off part-time in your community, and see what it is like. Do not try moving to any large market without experience. It is very expensive to live in New York, Los Angeles, Miami or Chicago, and they can be tough places to get started. If you already live in one of those markets, find small agencies to begin with.

You can get great tear sheets and lots of training and experience in your own community. If your area does not have much paid acting or modeling work, find a local college or university and audition for student films or create wonderful photos with photography students. After you have worked enough to get some strong pictures and a resume, have an agent help you create a comp card or at least a head shot. Once you have these materials, get copies made of your head shot/resume and then upload them to a website. After those projects are completed, then consider seeking work in a larger market.

I hope my stories and experience have given you a greater understanding and insight into the workings of the acting and commercial modeling industry. I hope your career brings you great satisfaction, as mine has for me. Good luck to you. Feel free to send me any industry-related questions. You can also watch my Acting and Modeling Quick Tip video blogs and other blog material on my website at www.howtoactandmodel.org.

If you would like additional information about my in-person workshops, online workshops, One-on-One online mentoring programs and my Tear Sheet *newsletter, email me at aaron@howtoactandmodel.com.*

Here are some additional ways to stay in touch with me:

My Website: www.howtoactandmodel.org
Friend me: www.facebook.com/howtomodel
Follow me on Twitter: www.twitter.com/aaronrmarcus
Follow me on Linkedin: www.linkedin.com/in/aaronrmarcus
Mentoring Program: http://howtoactandmodel.org/coaching

TWELVE
Now What Do You Do?

1. Take acting for the camera classes.

2. Take auditioning and improv classes and then begin auditioning for theater.

3. For modeling, practice getting different believable looks and expressions in front of a camera.

4. Do your homework and decide on your image.

5. Find a photographer and have your head shot taken.

6. Create strong commercial shots.

7. Print a few photos from your head shot session.

8. Create a "sample" comp card. Simply print two, three or four photos on a plain piece of paper with your name, stats and contact information.

9. Create a resume for your head shot.

10. Contact agents.

11. Once your photos have been selected, get your head shots and/or comp cards done by a professional printer.

12. If you have the time and interest, begin marketing yourself. Send your materials to photographers, art/creative directors at advertising agencies and casting directors.

13. Purchase and learn how to apply makeup.

14. Purchase equipment for home auditions.

THIRTEEN
Resources

Unions

AEA (www.actorsequity.org)
Actors' Equity Association (theater)
AEA is a mixture of an open and non-open union. If you are a member of a "sister" union, such as SAG-AFTRA, AGMA, AGVA or GIAA and you have met certain guidelines, then you can join AEA. The initiation fee is about $1,100, which can be paid over a period of time. And dues are paid twice a year, along with working dues, which are based on a small percentage of what you have earned. The other ways of joining AEA are to be cast in an equity play and offered an equity contract (this is similar to being cast as a principal actor in a SAG-AFTRA production), or to work in the Equity Membership Candidate Program (EMC) for 50 weeks in an equity play.

ACTRA (www.actra.ca/main)
Alliance of Canadian Cinema, Television and Radio Artists

SAG-AFTRA (www.sagaftra.org)
Screen Actors Guild – American Federation of Television and Radio Artists
To join, you must be cast as a principal character in a SAG-AFTRA production, get upgraded on a set, or work three days as an extra and be paid with a SAG-AFTRA voucher, or "cross over" from other SAG-AFTRA approved unions by fulfilling their specific requirements. The initiation fee is dependent on where you live. The most expensive initiation fee is about $3,100, but this number will vary depending on your market. The fees can frequently change, so check the SAG-AFTRA office nearest you to find the exact one-time initiation fee. Then, dues are paid twice a year based on a small percentage of your earnings.

Note: Since changes are always taking place with the unions, it is best to contact a union office for the most updated information.

Helpful Publications

The Marcus Institute's National Directory of SAG-AFTRA Offices
Published by The Marcus Institute
This valuable directory can help you find every Union office throughout the United States

The Marcus Institute's Industry Information Directory
This special directory gives you names and contact information of companies that print and reproduce head shots and composite sheets. You will also find a listing of great head shot photographers based in NY and LA. There is also an incredible list of websites that will help you find agents, managers, casting directors, photographers, free monologues and other industry related sites.

Each directory costs $15. Save $10 by purchasing both directories for only $20. Contact the Marcus Institute at aaron@howtoactandmodel.com or by phone at (410) 764-8270 for credit card orders.

The Marcus Institute's *Tear Sheet* Newsletter
Published by The Marcus Institute
This quarterly newsletter gives you incredible up-to-date information about the acting and modeling industry. Each issue has:
- A feature article with an industry professional
- Industry questions answered by Aaron Marcus
- Listings of our subscriber's latest classes, auditions and bookings (with contacts)
- Important acting and modeling websites
- A head shot evaluation by a photographer

Contact the Marcus Institute to subscribe.

Other Resources
One-on-One Online Mentoring Programs
http://howtoactandmodel.org/coaching
Aaron sets aside five days each month to work with people individually online.

Online Monthly Workshops
http://howtoactandmodel.org/workshops
Every month Aaron offers an amazing online workshop geared to both actors and models.

Season Pass Membership
http://howtoactandmodel.org/ (click on the link in the upper right hand corner)
With this membership you will save over 40 percent of the cost for attending and having access to every workshop that takes place that year.

Glossary of Terms

Ad:
Images and/or words used to help sell a product or idea.

Advertising agency:
Creates ad campaigns for clients. Sometimes selects the actors and models.

AEA
(Actors' Equity Association): Union for theater actors.

Agent:
A person who helps get actors and models work.

Art director:
Person who helps create and design ads.

Assistant photographer:
A person who helps a photographer before, during and after a photo session.

Backdrop:
The background used in the photographer's studio.

Base:
The first layer of makeup used on one's face.

Billboard:
A very large sign where ads are placed.

Body parts:
Some models are cast because of their special features, such as hands, feet, legs, hair, etc.

Bonus:
Payment of additional fees above the hourly or day rate. A bonus is received for a high-exposure ad, such as a poster, point of purchase, billboard or package, and long-term usage or exclusivity.

Book:
Another name for a portfolio.

Booking:
Getting hired for a job.

Booked out:
When you tell your agent that you are unavailable on certain dates.

Buy out:
Additional money is paid so the client can use the ad forever.

Call back:
When actors and models are called back to be seen again after the initial audition or go-see.

Call time:
The time the talent needs to be on the set.

Camera ready:
1. Art work that is ready for the printer.
2. When a model is ready to shoot with makeup and wardrobe on.

Cast:
Being hired for a job.

Casting:
When actors and models attend an audition or go-see to be seen for a project.

Casting director:
Person who auditions the talent and sometimes offers input on who should be cast.

Category:
A group of actors and models who have similar characteristics and features.

Catalog:
A book or magazine showing different products.

Cattle call:
When a large number of people attend a go-see or audition.

Cheating to the camera:
Slightly turning the head and eyesight away from the person or object the actor or model is working with and toward the camera lens. This technique gives the illusion that the talent is looking straight at the other person or object, and it allows the camera to see more of the person's face.

Client:
The company that hires the ad agency to have an ad produced.

Collection:
A group of coordinated clothing that is shown by a designer.

Commercial modeling:
Appearing in a still picture that promotes a product, or a company. People of all heights, ages and sizes can work as commercial models.

Commission:
A percentage of a model's earnings paid as a fee to an agent.

Composite sheet (comp or zed card):
A card showing the model's photos along with his or her statistics.

Conflict:
When a model has done an ad for a certain product, he or she avoids appearing in ads for competing products to avoid a conflict.

Copy:
The words of an ad.

Co-star:
Category for an actor who generally has a few lines and scenes in a project.

Copywriter:
Person who writes the words for an ad.

Creative director:
Person who creates the concept of the ad and sometimes determines which actor or model gets cast.

Crop:
To adjust the shape and size of a photo.

Digitals:
Current photos showing how the talent currently looks.

Direct booking:
Either when a model gets booked for a job without going through an agent, or having to attend a go-see.

Digital camera:
A camera that records pictures electronically instead of on film.

Editorial shot:
A photograph used to illustrate an article in a newspaper or magazine.

Exclusivity:
When a model is represented by only one agent.

Exclusivity fee:
Being paid to work for only one product or company.

Extra:
A model whose face is not clearly recognizable or is only seen in the background of a photo. In film or TV an actor who does not say any words.

Featured:
Category for someone who has a supporting role—not a lead, but a substantial part in the project.

Fee:
A monetary charge for a service.

Fit modeling:
Modeling a sample of the garment to test for sizing.

Freelancer:
Person who works with many agents or books jobs on his or her own.

Go-see:
The term used for job auditions for models.

Graphic artist:
Person who gets artwork ready for the printer.

Half body or 3/4 head shot:
A photograph that shows more of one's body than the typical head shot.

Head shot:
A close-up photo of a person's head from the chest up.

Indigo:
A reproduction process that is superior to lasers and inferior to printing.

Industrial film:
A training and/or educational film also known as a corporate film.

Job number:
A number assigned to an ad for billing and identification purposes.

Laser:
A copying process where toner is used to reproduce a photo.

Layout:
A sample concept of an ad, used for approval from the client and as a guide for the photographer.

Lead:
The main character or one of the main characters in the story.

Makeup artist:
Person who puts makeup on actors and models.

Mark:
Piece of tape on the floor showing the talent's position.

Mini book:
A small portfolio book with tear sheets and test shots of a model's work

Model form:
An information sheet that is filled out by models at a go-see.

Model release form:
A document giving a photographer or advertising agency full usage rights to a photo.

On location:
Shooting that takes place outside the photographer's studio or sound stage.

One-plus-one:
An hour-long booking with the possibility of working an additional hour.

Open call:
When an agent interviews new talent.

Photo credit:
The photographer's name next to his or her photo on your composite sheet.

Photomatic:
A slide or PowerPoint presentation.

Point of purchase:
A display ad in a store.

Polaroid:
A camera that produces a print in less then 60 seconds. Rarely used anymore.

Portfolio:
A compilation of a model's photos.

Powder:
Makeup used to take the shine off of one's face.

Prep time:
Time needed for special preparation before a session.

Print:
Term used for any photograph used in a printed format, such as catalogs, billboards, magazines, etc.

Print work:
Modeling jobs for all "still" shots. Ads for newspapers, products, Internet, posters, etc.

Profile:
The side view of the face or body.

Props:
Items used in a shot to make an ad look realistic.

Put on hold:
When a model or actor is asked to reserve a specific date for the possibility of being booked for a job.

Rates:
Term used for the fees the talent will receive.

Released:
When a model or actor is told he or she is no longer being considered for a job.

Request go-see:
When a model is specifically asked to appear for a casting.

Retouch:
To make a change on a photograph.

Right of first refusal:
When a talent has been put on hold and a second job is offered for the same day. The person who originally put the talent on hold has the right of first refusal. This person can either book or release the talent.

Scout:
A person searching for new talent.

SAG-AFTRA (Screen Actors Guild–American Federation of Television and Radio Artists):
Union for actors cast in movies, TV commercials, radio spots, music videos, narrations, TV programs, voice-overs, new media, interactives (video games), news and broadcasts, sound recordings, audio books and training films.

Session:
Another name for a print shoot or working on an acting job.

Shoot:
A photo session.

Sides:
The short portion of the script that is read for TV and film auditions.

Sign-in sheet:
Sheet of paper for models to write their names and some additional information. It is used at go-sees so everyone knows who is next in line to have a photo taken. And, can be used at acting auditions.

Square to the camera:
When a model's face and body are facing straight into the lens.

Stats:
Information used listing the talent's height, weight, hair/eye color, clothing sizes, etc.

Stock photography:
Generic photographs that can be rented to companies for ad campaigns.

Stylist:
Person responsible for assembling wardrobe and sometimes props for a job.

Submittance:
When agents send photos in the hopes of getting auditions and or bookings for their talent.

Tear sheet:
A copy of an ad.

Test shot:
A photo used solely for a photographer's or model's portfolio.

Trade magazine:
A publication marketed to a specific field.

Trade shows:
Events normally held at hotels or convention centers where companies promote products/services.

Transit:
Posters on vehicles, such as buses or subways.

Transparent apparel:
Clothing that can be seen through.

Travel reimbursement:
When a talent is refunded the money spent for transportation to a shoot.

Travel time:
Getting paid for traveling. This can occur when a talent travels a long distance getting to a job.

Type face:
The size and style of letters used in printing.

Upgrade:
When an ad is placed in a high-exposure format and the model receives an additional fee. Or when a talent is promoted to a more prominent role in a project.

Usage:
How and where the ad will run.

Voucher:
The bill/invoice and contract that is used in the modeling industry.

Wardrobe:
Clothes that are used at a photo session.

Weather permit:
A job on location that is dependent on good weather can be cancelled. Details will be worked out by the agent.

About the Author

Aaron Marcus has been a full-time actor and commercial model for over 30 years. He has been cast in over 1,200 acting and modeling projects. Aaron has worked on commercial projects for companies such as Disney World, Molson Beer, Colonial Williamsburg, Discovery Channel, NEA, Citicorp, Crayola Crayons, Proctor & Gamble, Nissan, Ikea, AT&T, McDonald's, StarKist Tuna, Acura, Harrah's Casino, Showtime, Campbell's, The Learning Channel, LifeSavers, Guinness Gold, United Way, Western Union, Red Roof Inn, Hertz, K-Mart, Nationwide Insurance and Coca-Cola. His commercial modeling ads have appeared throughout the United States, Canada, Europe, The Netherlands and Asia and have been seen in magazines such as *Time, People, Maxim, Reader's Digest, The New York Times, Parents, Forbes, TV Guide, Sports Illustrated, Money, Newsweek* and *The Wall Street Journal*.

Aaron Marcus has been cast on TV and in films such as *Gotham, House of Cards, Rectify, Do No Harm, The Wire, Halt and Catch Fire, Philomena, America's Most Wanted, Homicide, Life on the Street, Eugene, A Modest Suggestion, Project Almanac, The West Wing* and *Law & Order: Criminal Intent*.

He has worked on corporate films for companies and organizations such as AAA, AARP, Armstrong Floors, Gannett Corporation, IBM, IRS, DIA, Lockheed Martin, Lucent Technologies, National School Board Association, New Holland, Pitney Bowes, CIA, the Pentagon, U.S.D.A., U.S. Navy and USPS.

Along with his modeling and acting, Aaron Marcus was a faculty member of the School for Film and Television in New York, and he has written articles for Women In Film (LA and Baltimore branches), *Clique Magazine*/Canada, *New Generation Magazine*/London, The Actors' Center, The Models Guild, International Television Association, Icom and the Screen Actors Guild. Aaron was interviewed by Judy Kerr in her book *Acting Is Everything*, for Nancy Heubeck's book *Career for Kids* and for *The Modeling Handbook* by Eve Matheson. Aaron publishes the *Tear Sheet* newsletter, which is a quarterly publication devoted to the acting and commercial modeling industry. He also is the founder of the Marcus Institute, www.howtoactandmodel.org, which presents free acting and modeling video blogs.

Aaron has given his "Book the Job" acting and modeling workshop over 600 times, spanning three continents. Along with offering his workshops to the general public, he also gives them at acting/modeling schools, colleges, organizations and talent agencies.

Aaron Marcus also offers monthly online workshops at http://howtoactandmodel.org/workshops, as well as private One-on-One online programs at http://howtoactandmodel.org/coaching. To see the recorded online workshops, visit http://howtoactandmodel.org and click on the Store link. For additional information about Aaron's workshops and private sessions, contact The Marcus Institute at (410) 764-8270 or visit http://howtoactandmodel.org.